Praise for *Raise Your Love Signal*

"This book is a must for anyone looking to attract and keep an incredible partner. Chantal takes the reader on a journey to better understand themselves, how they show up in relationships, as well as how to find, and create the relationship they have always dreamt of. She provides simple steps and simple questions that will leave you with more confidence to raise your love signal and call the partnership of your dreams. It's deep, straight-up truth and easy to follow."

MARK GROVES Speaker, Writer, Motivator and Founder of Create The Love

"This book is an inspiring and practical guide to getting the love you want. Whether you are single or in a relationship that needs to grow, you will get step-by-step coaching from a woman who has courageously forged her own path. Chantal will teach you to raise your love signal!"

TANYA CHERNOVA Inspiring Global Speaker, #1 Best-Selling Author

"If you're looking for an in-depth, comprehensive guide for attracting/finding/keeping the love of your life, *Raise Your Love Signal* is for you. This book is deliciously and densely packed with insights, exercises and proven methods of self-reflection that are essential to 'doing the work' to discover what you need to do, if love is what you want. Most engaging are the personal stories of clients Chantal has worked with and their breakthroughs to finding lasting romantic love Landreville's own 'deep dives' into her personal story, exploring with great vulnerability the struggles she grappled with and overcame to find passionate, deep and compelling love with her partner. It's a love story and also a guidebook on how to make your very own love story. *Raise Your Love Signal* is the real deal. It's like walking into the gym on January 1st; be prepared to do the work and the results you achieve will be far beyond your expectations."

RON GERBLER Producer

RAISE YOUR
LOVE
SIGNAL

A Guide to Attracting and
Keeping the Love of Your Life

CHANTAL LANDREVILLE

GRAMMAR
FACTORY
— EST. 2013 —

Grammar Factory Publishing
MacMillan Company Limited
25 Telegram Mews, 39th Floor,
Suite 3906
Toronto, Ontario, Canada
M5V 3Z1

www.grammarfactory.com

Landreville, Chantal
Raise Your Love Signal: A Guide to Attracting and Keeping the Love of Your Life / Chantal Landreville.

Paperback ISBN 978-1-998756-56-8
Hardcover ISBN 978-1-998756-58-2
eBook ISBN 978-1-998756-57-5

1. FAM029000 FAMILY & RELATIONSHIPS / Love & Romance. 2. FAM030000 FAMILY & RELATIONSHIPS / Marriage & Long-Term Relationships. 3. SEL023000 SELF-HELP / Personal Growth / Self-Esteem.

Production Credits
Cover design by Marie-Judith Jean-Louis
Interior layout design by Setareh Ashrafologhalai
Book production and editorial services by Grammar Factory Publishing

Grammar Factory's Carbon Neutral Publishing Commitment
Grammar Factory Publishing is proud to be neutralizing the carbon footprint of all printed copies of its authors' books printed by or ordered directly through Grammar Factory or its affiliated companies through the purchase of Gold Standard-Certified International Offsets.

CONTENTS

INTRODUCTION
WHAT DOES IT MEAN
TO RAISE YOUR
LOVE SIGNAL?

I F YOU'VE picked up this book, chances are you've had your share of struggles in the love department. Maybe you're single and are desperately seeking your life partner. Maybe you're wondering why you keep attracting the wrong men. You might just be coming out of a toxic relationship or are discontented with your current relationship and ready to throw in the towel.

You want to do something about it, but . . .

- you hate online dating and feel frustrated by how hard it is to meet "the one",

- you put yourself out there but keep attracting low-quality, emotionally unavailable men,

- you fear the idea that your clock is ticking,

- you think you're doing everything right or just can't figure out what you are doing wrong,

- you worry you'll never find love, that it will never happen for you.

Basically, you are sick and tired of the entire subject and feel hopeless.

Well, guess what? You're not alone. That is why I know this book is right for you. It will not only help you understand all these feelings, it will also help you in your search to attract the Love of your Life.

Believe me, I have personally experienced all of these issues. Every. Single. One. I know exactly how you feel. Every tear you've shed, every moment of depression and loneliness you've experienced, every ounce of self-doubt and anger you feel . . . I've been there. And like you, I have asked myself more than once, "What is wrong with me? Why is this not happening for me? Will I ever find love or what my heart truly desires?"

You see, I was a single gal, too, alone for more than fifteen years and struggling in all the areas of finding love as you are. The good news, and, yes, there is good news, is that all those tears I shed got me here, writing this book that will hopefully transform your love life.

Now, you might be wondering why I'm so fascinated with love, with dating and relationships. My father's passing when I was two years old certainly affected me deeply and had a lot to do with it. Of course, I didn't know this at the time, but I'm sure it affected my need for male attention, which I'll tell you more about as we continue. For now, I'll say I am sure this need developed into the idea of being in love with "being in love". I would fantasize about romance, about my prince charming and how he would sweep me off my feet to live the *happily-ever-after* life, just like in a Disney movie.

Sadly, life isn't a Disney love story. For most of my adult life I was light years away from that. All my attempts at love failed, leaving me with so much hurt, rejection, and disappointment. It led me to a dark place. I started questioning myself: "Is there something wrong with me? Am I being too demanding? Am I not loveable enough?"

Or, the worst one: "Will I be alone for the rest of my life?" (Reading this sentence today, it makes me sad that once upon a time I actually thought this, and lived in fear about it.)

Self-doubt crept into my head without my even realizing it. I started to question my self-worth (I literally thought I was not worthy of love). When I reflect on those dark days, I shudder to think what I had to go through to get to where I am today. Hopefully, your being here can help you avoid that journey.

But, then, every journey has a beginning and these experiences were my initiation to the world of self-development and personal growth. And, as with every journey, this meant I needed to do the work on myself to find and attract my life partner. This demanded some soul-searching and a deeper dive to get to the root of why I wasn't able to attract and keep my right partner for a long-term, committed relationship. I also needed to recognize patterns in my life and understand why I had them.

So, I started reading. I became almost addicted to reading and researching everything that was out there about relationships, male-female connections, human behaviour, and everything in between. I was also lucky enough to have numerous guides, friends, and angels who helped me along the way by giving me the right advice and pointing me in the right direction in terms of books, self-help conferences, healers, life coaches, Vipassana meditation practices, Ayahuasca ceremonies, Tantra workshops, retreats, and many other experiences.

At one point, though, I realized I needed to stop consuming. I had officially become a self-help junkie, learning and discovering all these things but not applying any of them to my own personal life, which was why nothing was really changing for me. It's one thing to learn; it's a whole other to apply the lessons and use the tools and skills acquired along the way (keep this in mind as you work through this book and start making the changes you need to, and remember as well that deep beliefs and patterns set in our brain for more than twenty, thirty, or forty years do not change overnight). You know that old saying, that doing the same thing over and over again but expecting different results is the definition of insanity? Well, more than anything, it's unrealistic.

The good news is that with twenty years of accumulated knowledge, and the associated wisdom I've gained along the way, what I learned about the most was myself. For that alone, I wouldn't change any of the lousy men I dated or the pain and struggles I experienced. As it turns out, I just had to reprogram my mindset and not allow myself to be defined by past experiences.

In fact, I truly believe I had to go through everything I've been through to write this book and be the guide I am today. I Raised my Love Signal to the highest level. Now, my mission is to help you raise yours, to help you find the love you deserve so you can be in a happy, healthy, long-term, committed relationship (and hopefully save yourself twenty years of misery).

And, no, the journey won't be all sunshine and rainbows. There will be learning curves. There will be a lot of kicking and screaming, tears, and pain. But it will pay off. I promise. Not only have I been able to attract my dream life partner, I also discovered a deep love for myself—one that I had never experienced before.

And, there's even more great news—you are not alone in this journey towards love. There are so many of us on this path willing to share our stories. That's how, through my years of studying this subject and talking to and coaching other women, I've come to recognize three main concerns about looking for love:

1 **Most women think they are ready for love.** Yet, as we explore why we struggle to find and keep it, we realize we're not. At root, we often don't feel worthy of receiving it, not the high-quality man or the relationship we dream of. The question then is "How can I attract a high-quality partner if I don't feel worthy of receiving him, and if I can't open up that space for love?"

2 **Leading from this first point is the idea that we are afraid of being hurt.** We create a barrier as a defense, a cement wall. How can you fall in love when there's a cement wall around your heart? It's then we realize we haven't dealt with other issues, like unresolved traumas and/or past hurts that can significantly impact our future relationships—I myself had no awareness of my own emotional triggers or how to communicate them, which meant I was a disaster in all of my new short-term relationships. This leads many of us to have trust issues, to maintain an emotional distance or develop co-dependencies, negative coping mechanisms, communication difficulties, and conflict avoidance. None of these things will lead to successful relationships. All of this just further highlights the importance of doing the healing work.

3 **Many of us are in love with the idea of love and of falling in love.** Yet, we don't fully understand What does it mean to "be in" Love and to sustain a relationship beyond all the rom-com/Disney-like scenarios we create in our heads? We have never been taught anything about it, especially how "to be" in a relationship and what it takes to make one succeed.

This last one really got me thinking. Every single human being on the face of the Earth desires and deserves love and to be loved, regardless of place, religion, culture, or colour. It is a universal emotion. So how can something so important to humankind not be part of our education system? We go to school to learn about mathematics, geography, languages, and science, even religion for some of us (says the former Catholic schoolgirl). Why are we not taught social skills like communication, emotional intelligence, and self-worth and confidence building? Wouldn't some form of "love education" taught to us from a young age help us grow and become better partners, better parents, better friends?

One doesn't become an athlete overnight. It takes years of practice, skill building, and working with a coach. Actually, anything you want to become an expert in, any field you want to thrive in, demands the same thing. Yet, we are expected to navigate through love, dating, and relationships, and even raise kids with no tools given to us and no lessons taught to us whatsoever. We have to wing it! How can society expect any of us to succeed?

It's time we change our way of thinking and perceiving love. It's time we stop repeating the patterns that have been passed down to us from previous generations. It's time we open our minds to learn and integrate new ways of approaching love.

I have made it my mission to show people the proper love connection skills not only to attract the right partner, but also to create and stay in a fun, joyful, long-lasting, healthy relationship, both with yourself and with your partner. Yes, you read that right. With yourself. A healthy relationship needs to start with you. When you understand your own needs and boundaries, build your self-esteem and confidence, and cultivate self-love. When you are fulfilled from within, only then will you be a good, strong partner. Only then will you be able to enter into relationships from a place of authenticity, respect, and mutual understanding.

Throughout this book, I will share more of my personal story to show you how I learned to love myself so that I could learn to love others, how I stepped into my power as a woman and raised my worth to a whole other level. I'll share with you what I've learned from the experts, the readings, and all the resources that are out there so that this Guide to Attracting and Keeping the Love of Your Life will enable you to view love in a whole new way. Think of it as a master's degree in love.

By the time you're done reading, you will have covered three Love Lessons:

1   Your Wants
2   Your Self
3   You in the Relationship

The ultimate goal? If you practice just a little of the lessons presented in this book, you will absolutely never settle for just anyone or for a bad relationship ever again. Instead, you will be equipped and ready to . . .

- attract the right partner for you

- be clear on the kind of relationship you want to grow and evolve in

- know your worth and develop self-confidence

- be the true You and not compromise your authentic self

- identify your boundaries and learn how to stick to them

- know how to deal with your past wounds and not drag your past baggage or old patterns into your new relationship

- understand your triggers and how to deal with them when they surface

- become a great communicator

- learn how to date the right way

- absorb the key tools to help you to navigate your relationship in a healthy way

Of course, you can't discount your own life experiences as sources of valuable lessons. However, having the right knowledge and awareness definitely helps you go through the motions faster. In other words, you don't have to suffer through a bad relationship after five years when you should and could end it after five months. It shouldn't take three dates to realize you are being mistreated and that you should say goodbye after one.

Knowledge is power. The more you know, the easier your journey to love will be. Empower yourself! Let me empower you. Let's Raise Your Love Signal and get you the Love of your Life!

YOUR WANTS

WELCOME TO your first Love Lesson—Your Wants.

First, ask yourself why you're here. It's probably because you *want* to find love, you *want* to be "in love", and you *want* to be in a relationship. You also most likely *want* to know why these *wants* are not being met, right?

Well, it's time you discover what it is you "think" you want and how to go about finding love and being "in love". In the next few chapters, we'll look at how getting a clear grasp on your *wants* can help you find and attract the right partner and sustain a healthy relationship without losing yourself in it.

1

WHAT IS LOVE, ANYWAY?

GOOD QUESTION, RIGHT?
It was the one question I couldn't really answer for myself even after all the work I had done, after all the books I had read, and after learning everything about it I could over the past twenty years. How could the average person answer this question? How could we answer this question if we've never been taught about love or about how to be in a relationship?

In this chapter, I define love and explain why it's important for you to assess your own current definition of it. Doing this will help you have more clarity on how you want to grow and evolve in a relationship. Thankfully, my own curiosity led me to explore all the layers behind the subject... because that's exactly what they are, layers. There are so many of them, and they are not all easy to understand and navigate through on your own. In fact, you might not even be aware of all the different things you can learn about love.

At first, I wasn't sure how I could help other women in this respect. I didn't know how I could pass on my understanding of this topic to them. So, I decided to go straight to the source—I went to you beautiful ladies. I did tons of surveys, and I organized coffee table talks with groups of women to ask them about all things love and what they felt they needed to know more about to help them do better in matters of the heart. Everything in this book is a curation and summation of that research, as well as some of my own insights gained through practice and my journey to a beautiful place with myself and my relationship with my life partner.

So, the first question I always ask women is, "How do you define love?"

To hear every woman answer from such a different perspective was just fascinating. It really shows how many layers love actually has. This was the strongest confirmation I had yet that none of us grew up learning about love. We just experienced it first-hand through our parents (for better or worse) and then through the natural flow of life: desiring it, yearning for it, searching for it, loving it, failing at it, and getting hurt by it. All the while, we were just "figuring it out".

A Definition of Love

So, what is Love, anyway?

As per Webster's Dictionary, here are a few technical definitions[1]:

As a noun:

1 a feeling of strong or constant affection for a person

2 an attraction that includes sexual desire: the strong affection felt by people who have a romantic relationship

3 a person you love in a romantic way

---

1 Merriam-Webster. "Love." Merriam-Webster Dictionary. https://www.merriam-webster.com/dictionary/love.

As a verb:

1   to hold dear
2   to feel a lover's passion, devotion, or tenderness
3   to like or desire actively; take pleasure in

Love can have many meanings and be so many different things in different contexts. There is not a right or a wrong answer, nor a single definition. Think about it; love can bring you peace, love can calm you down, love can make you feel safe, love can make you smile and feel good all over. Love can also hurt; it can be painful and toxic. Love can be with a partner, but it can also be with our children, our friends, our family members, and our co-workers. There are all kinds of love for different people and different situations.

One thing disturbed me, however. Neither the numerous groups of women I spoke with, nor the dictionary, made any mention of love for the self. That's when I realized we've been programmed, as a society, to make love about everyone else but ourselves. We are told how love needs to function in our lives, that it should be catered to the external—outside of us, not within us. To me, love starts with myself. Only then, can I love another. The same is true for everyone else.

Sadly, though, this was a hard lesson I didn't appreciate until later in life, and it was one of the reasons I couldn't attract the right relationship. If I did not have love for myself as a person, how could I receive it from a man? But, the topic of self-love deserves a chapter of its own, so I'll get back to this in Chapter 6.

The first key to love

Just as important as having self-love, I've come to understand how important it is for you to know what *you* want *your* relationship with love to be. That is because you can only receive love in the same way you "think" you know how to give it.

You can only receive love in the same way you "think" you know how to give it. (This feels like such a powerful statement, I wanted to write it twice.)

If your current relationship with love is characterized by mistrust, hurt, or anger, you will continue attracting toxic relationships because it's what you associate with love in your subconscious mind. In contrast, when you take the time to understand what love really means for you and what you want it to be, you will not only attract the right type of love but you will also be able to notice the red flags when it isn't right for you. By getting clear on what love means for you, you will more easily receive it when it shows up. It will also help you stick to and stick up for your needs by allowing you to set your boundaries and not settle.

When we know what we want our relationship with love to be, we completely change what kind of relationship/partners we attract and are much more straightforward about staying true to who we are.

So how do you honour your desires? Ask yourself these questions:

- How do I want love to manifest for me?

- How do I want it to make me feel?

- How do I want to give it to others? Am I willing to invest 100% towards another person?

- How do I want to receive it?

If you want to be in a healthy relationship you need to get very clear on what all these attributes mean to you. The less clear you are, the less likely you are to succeed and more likely to continue to attract love for the wrong reasons.

What is your relationship with love?

This is the second question I ask my clients when we start working together.

These two questions (How do you define love? and What is your relationship to love?) might sound silly, even flaky, but the answers don't often come easy when you really take the time to reflect on them. In fact, this simple reflective exercise is usually quite eye-opening for my clients.

Think about it; if your relationship with love so far has always been about giving, at some point you will need to learn how to receive it. If your relationship with love has always been about accommodating your partners and not staying true to who you really are, you will need to set your boundaries and learn to stay true to the real you. If your relationship with love is such that you do not feel worthy of receiving it, how will you ever attract a high-quality man?

Do you see how the big picture comes together here?

To understand what or how you need to change, what you need to ask for, and what you need to pay attention to when you are dating, you first need to know what your relationship with love is and who you need to become to receive it. In Chapter 2, we will look in greater depth at identifying your needs and wants, as well as behaviours that didn't work for you in past relationships so that you don't repeat them.

Remember, a relationship is a two-way street. It's not all about me—my needs, my wants. If you want to be in a healthy partnership, then you need to know how to "show up" for it, how to be present and active in the relationship. A healthy relationship is one in which two people equally have the willingness and desire to take care of each other's needs for the relationship's best interest.

SARAH'S STORY

Sarah was a successful career woman in her late thirties. After a string of failed relationships, she decided to seek my help. The first thing I did was ask her two questions: "How do you define love?" and "What is your relationship with love?"

Reflecting, Sarah realized that she had always approached love from a perspective of giving, often neglecting her own needs and desires in the process. She had accommodated her partners while compromising her authenticity and setting aside her own boundaries. She also realized that deep down, she didn't feel worthy of receiving love, which led to her attracting partners who were not emotionally available or committed to a healthy, loving relationship.

Through our work together, Sarah gained clarity on what she truly wanted from a loving partnership and who she needed to become to receive it. Over time, Sarah's mindset and approach to love transformed. She gained confidence and learned to receive love from feeling worthy.

Armed with her newfound insights and self-awareness, Sarah began to approach dating with a fresh perspective. She set clear expectations for herself and communicated her needs and boundaries to potential partners. She also learned to listen to her intuition and pay attention to red flags, all of which helped her make healthier choices in her dating life.

As a result, she attracted a high-quality man who appreciated her authenticity and respected her boundaries. They built a healthy, loving, long-term relationship based on mutual respect, communication, and shared values.

She realized that understanding her relationship with love and showing up authentically were crucial for building healthy, fulfilling relationships. She learned that love is not just about giving, but also about receiving and taking care of one's own needs.

Summary

Hopefully, by now you understand that I am on a mission to show you some very different ways of thinking about yourself and about love so you can change what hasn't worked for you in your love life so far. Taking the time to ask yourself "What is love?", and "What is my relationship with love?" will give you so much insight you never realized was right in front of you the whole time. If nothing else, you will at least form a clear idea of what love means to *you* now.

RAISE YOUR LOVE SIGNAL

Find some time to sit down in a quiet space, and journal about these two questions:

1   How do you define love?
2   What is your relationship with love?

Write down as many details as you can. Refer back to old, failed relationships and ask yourself: How would love show up for me today knowing what I know now? How will it be different for me and the relationship going forward? What will I accept now, and what will I not?

Also write down your "Ah-ha" moment, or that moment you realized something wasn't working for you in past relationships and what triggered that realization. Another "Ah-ha" moment can be when you realize something about yourself that has changed your views on love and/or relationships.

2

KNOWING WHAT
YOU WANT

OW THAT you have gotten a handle on your relationship
with love, let's start working on getting a clear vision
of what you want from your partner and the actual
relationship. This begins by learning to distinguish between
your *wants* and your *needs*. By identifying these two vital
points, you'll get closer to knowing what really matters to you.

Do you even know what you want?

Let's start with this simple question.

You're probably saying, "Of course, I know what I want."
And I'm sure you "think" you do. Most women do.

That is until I ask them to describe their vision of a relationship. I do this by breaking it down into two parts:

1. What do you want from your partner?
This is the easiest part. It breaks the dam, opens them up and
lets the ideas flow like water. Every woman is really great at
describing what she wants, and doesn't want, from a partner.

Try it yourself. Here is an important exercise to help you get crystal clear about what you want from a partner. Consider these attributes and say out loud or write down what aspects you want your partner to satisfy in terms of each:

- Physicality
- Emotions
- Intimacy
- Common interests
- Education
- Values

Knowing what you want in a partner physically and emotionally is indeed important, but there is much more to the success of a relationship than looks and personality. Being with a good-looking guy who's into sports and loves to cook does not commonly set the foundation for your relationship to build on and survive in the long run. So let's ask the next question:

2. What do you want from your relationship?

This part gets a little more complicated, and every woman struggles with it. Unlike their clear ideas about a partner, ideas about the relationship become vague, unfocused.

"What do you mean?" my clients will ask.

Have you thought about your vision of what your relationship should look like? Or how you see yourself growing and evolving as a couple?

Imagine your ideal relationship. Now, ask yourself these questions:

- How do you feel in your relationship? (safe, insecure, happy, anxious, inspired, etc.)

- How does he support you?

- How does it feel when he touches you?

- How do you both show up for each other in conflict?

- Do you share the same value system?

- What is your communication like?

And there it is, that deer-in-the-headlights stare. "I never thought about it that way. I've never even thought about these things. I guess I don't really know what I want."

That's just it! Every single woman I've ever worked with reacts in the same way.

We are really good at thinking about what we want and don't want in a partner, but we don't take the time to ask ourselves in-depth questions about what we *need* in order to sustain a long-term committed relationship. But that's ultimately what we want, right?

First of all, remember that this isn't your fault. We've never been taught to think about these things. The only thing we've been taught about love and relationships is the romance of it. The fantasy of finding the right partner and falling in love. The "oohs" and "ahs", the butterflies in the stomach, the "I can't wait to see you again" excitement. The lust and the passion. Yet, we've been taught absolutely nothing about the tools and values we need to succeed in a relationship.

I can't stress enough how important the above exercise is in your quest to understanding what the right relationship means to you. I urge you to think deeply and identify your wants and your needs as they apply to both your partner and the relationship you desire. Asking yourself these questions will open your eyes and mind to a whole other dimension of love.

Wants versus needs

There is a massive difference between what you want and need in a partner, just as there is between what you want and need from your relationship. Let's start with your Wants.

Wants

We are really good at expressing what we want. For example: I want him to be tall, and have great hair. I want him to cook. I want him to be funny, to dance, to be financially stable. I want him to be educated, a world traveller. I want him to be a great lover. And so on.

I want, I want, I want ... Sound familiar?

Wants are typically superficial and concentrated on the self. But we forget that a relationship is not all about the self, that it involves two people. Well, three entities, actually: you, your partner, and the union of the two—the relationship itself. A fabulous threesome.

Yes, the relationship is an entity on its own. It is two individuals coming together to create and make decisions on what is best for the union at all times, not just for the two of you as separate individuals. Unfortunately, society has programmed us to think of the individual first and foremost. Well, it's time to take control of your own program (more on that in the last chapter).

Then, of course, there are your needs. But before we go on to talk about our *needs*, consider Amber's story.

AMBER'S STORY

At thirty-one years old, Amber was very clear about what she wanted from her future partner—a world traveller, charming, driven, wanting kids, financially successful. It took her a few years, but she finally met and attracted the man of her dreams. He had everything she had *wanted*.

However, while her now ex-husband Bill was indeed very well off, it came at a high price. He was away for work for weeks at a time, leaving her alone to handle their two kids. When he was around, he was not very present, always felt tired and didn't want to do anything. Their visions and values on things like how to bring up their kids didn't align, which created a lot of friction and, inevitably, fights. Bill had difficulties communicating and would often simply leave, yet again, on a business trip instead of dealing with his reality.

Despite all this, Amber had a great life, with a big house, a fancy car, designer bags, and so on. But she felt alone in her relationship. She was miserable and so were her kids. This led to resentment, anger, miscommunication, and, finally, even infidelity.

I worked with Amber two years after she divorced. When discussing her vision for the new relationship she wanted, I asked her to explain why her marriage had failed and what her vision had been back then.

Looking back now, she realizes how shallow and egotistical she had been with her wants. "Appearance and lifestyle were important to me back then. Needless to say, it came back to bite me on the ass. I wanted things for the wrong reasons. I never took the time to understand what my needs were versus my wants and how that could impact my relationship in the long run."

Amber was ready to do things differently this time around. She had *wanted* all these amazing, superficial things, but over the long term of their relationship, these things didn't matter. The relation-ship didn't develop, didn't work. Her fundamental needs weren't being met. What did develop were feelings of loneliness and anger because she wasn't getting the physical and emotional presence she needed from her husband. She *needed* someone who made her and the family a priority versus someone who compensated by buy-ing expensive gifts to show his love.

She *needed* a man who could communicate, who could show up during hardships, who could deal with conflict instead of fleeing. Bill simply didn't know how to provide other than financially. Being emotional and understanding just wasn't part of his DNA. Worse, he'd never been that person from the start, but Amber had con-vinced herself he would change with time.

So, was the *want* of having a rich, successful man really the right reason for her to have a relationship with him? It sure wasn't. But this happens often when women look for love. We do not take the time to think about what it would really take to grow and evolve with this person, or to discover the fundamental needs that will help us succeed once the passion, the lust, the butterflies, or simply the fantasy of the new shiny object syndrome pass.

We get caught up in the fantasy of finding our person and fall in love with that *idea*. Trust me, I know all about it; it's happened to me more than once.

We must understand that *wants* can come at a very high price if we don't take the time to also think about our *needs* and how they serve us separately from our partner and the actual relationship.

Speaking of *Needs*...

Your *needs* refer to the fundamentals, the values or demands you have that come very close to being deal-breakers. In other words, these *needs* are the things you would never tolerate or accept in a relationship, and they leave no room for compromise; these can include, for example, your partner being a non-smoker, or concepts like a sense of security, confidence, trust, fidelity.

Needs also determine how you will provide for one another. Remember—a successful, quality relationship consists of two people coming together and being willing to take care of each other's needs. It's about how each of you wants to be taken care of, supported, and listened to. In many cases, though, we seem to think it's OK to make it all about *our* needs and wants without even thinking about how we will actually serve *our partner*'s needs in the relationship. To have your wants and needs met, you have to actively reciprocate these.

Again, you are in a threesome: you, your partner, and the relationship. To best serve this union, learn to question your wants and needs individually and pay attention to how they are different.

Also, keep in mind that we often limit our ability to meet really great men because we get caught up in our superficial *wants* rather than our fundamental relationship *needs*. Or worse, we convince ourselves we want or need certain things because we have been conditioned by our caregivers to think this way. Always remember that nobody knows you as you do. Listening to what *you* need and want is the most important. Parents undoubtedly have the best intentions, because they want the very best for us, but they cannot control who you are or will be and they certainly cannot control how you will grow in your relationships.

Of course, there's more to it than that. But we'll consider deal-breakers and their root causes in the next chapter.

Your long-term vision

If you want a long-term, committed relationship, it is crucial you put some thought into your long-term goals. Romance, flirting, good sex, and the excitement of a new relationship will come and go. Yet, knowing how you will both navigate the years beyond is a far more serious thing. You need to have a vision of the kind of relationship you see yourself growing in, evolving in, and living through every day, like a steady ship crossing the ocean of life, including all its ups and downs.

You see, it's easy to lose ourselves in excitement, especially when we meet someone we like. We can quickly excuse behaviours we would never tolerate otherwise, or start compromising our own needs to please another. As you start dating, keep the exercises in this book in mind as they will help you stay sharp when dealing with the potential partners you meet and avoid getting lost in the fantasy and romance aspect of it. Learn to pay attention to the red flags, the green flags, accept what really matters, and maybe even let go some of your *wants* because your *needs* are being met.

So, to help you continue to reflect on the differences between your *wants* and *needs*, here are a few questions you should ask yourself:

- How do I want to be treated or cared for in my relationship?

- How do I want to deal with things as a couple when we get into fights?

- How do I want my partner to show up if I get sick or have to deal with a family crisis?

- How can I provide for my partner?

- How do I want to raise kids together (for example, agreeing on religion, values, etc.)?

- What fundamental values do I want us to share?

- What are common goals I want to have with my partner?

- What are my deal-breakers (non-negotiables)?

MY STORY

When I was single, one of my *wants* was to be with a partner who could dance.

Dancing is a huge passion of mine. I could dance anywhere, anytime as long as the tunes are good. I always had a vision in my head that when I met my match, we would take salsa classes together, kill the dance floor at weddings and parties, and even get down at home in the kitchen being silly.

When I met Jeff, I still remember asking him, "Do you dance?" His answer: "I wish I could say yes, but I have two left feet."

Ugh! I still recall the disappointment in my head. "This isn't possible," I thought. So, I continued: "Do you at least have rhythm?"

"What do you mean?"

"Can you beep and bop your hips or do some sort of shoulder roll?" (I was desperate, OK?)

"I can raise my two hands up and down in the air but that's the extent of it."

I can't tell you how devastated I was, but as we got to know each other a little more, he was checking so many other boxes that really mattered to me.

Here is one among my list of *needs*: I need a man who is supportive and accepts me, that encourages me in everything I love to do. As it turns out, anytime I do want to go dancing, Jeff is completely understanding and is happy to see me go out dancing with my friends because he knows how happy it makes me. He encourages me to do it. He'll even make the effort to join me on the dance floor with his hands up in the air at a wedding or a party (after a couple shots of tequila, of course).

Having my partner being able to dance was a huge *want*. It wasn't a *need*. Dancing is not how we would've survived together as a couple through the ups and down. Support, acceptance, and respect for what I love definitely is.

Summary

Let's review some key aspects on your quest to find your partner:

- Get clear on what you *want* and *need* from your partner and your relationship.

- Create your long-term vision for your relationship.

It is important to be clear on your *wants* and *needs* and drill down into your vision because what you want and what you actually need are very different things.

And remember this as well: to attract the relationship of your dreams, you need to be damn clear on what that means to you. If there is any trace of confusion or uncertainty, the universe can't provide. It's as confused and uncertain as you are.

RAISE YOUR LOVE SIGNAL

I absolutely love this exercise:

Create a vision board of your relationship.[2]

Vision boards are much more than inspirational collages that form a picture of your future. They allow our brains to respond very strongly to visual stimulation, making our visualizations even more powerful. We create them so that we can have our goals and dreams become even clearer, and this lets us work more easily towards making them happen.

Vision boards can be done with a simple DIY creation. Have fun with it. Cut out pictures from your favourite magazines, print them out from Pinterest mood boards, or anywhere else. Create the relationship and your life together on the board.

---

2   A vision board is like a visual roadmap of your dreams and goals. It's a collage you create using pictures, words, and images that represent what you want to achieve in life, helping you stay focused and motivated to reach those aspirations. See examples:

www.oprahdaily.com/life/a29959841/how-to-make-a-vision-board/
www.jackcanfield.com/blog/vision-board/

3

KNOWING
YOUR *WHY*

IN THIS CHAPTER, let's figure out if you want what you want for the right reasons. We'll start by evaluating why deal-breakers are important and where they typically stem from. We'll also discuss who you need to become to attract that special partner. That's because it's not just about attracting the right person, it's also about working on preparing ourselves to receive him. Finally, we'll explore how you want to feel in your relationship. Remember, feeling it … is manifesting it.

Knowing the why behind your wants

Before we look at our wants, let's consider deal-breakers and where they come from. As we discussed in the previous chapter, your needs can basically be considered deal-breakers. Let's take that conversation a step further.

Needs that are non-negotiable are often rooted in a past trauma or a bad experience. When I talk about trauma, it doesn't need to be something awful like abuse, rape, or death; it could be something simpler, like never being heard when you talked or tried to voice an opinion, or being humiliated when expressing a hidden passion, or facing rejection when dating.

Since traumas are experiences that leave us feeling deeply unsafe or helpless, we want to make sure they don't happen again, which helps explain why we create deal-breakers to defend against them. To illustrate what I mean, here are a few classic examples of deal-breakers that could be related to past traumas:

- **Fidelity**—you were cheated on in a past relationship(s).

- **Financial security**—you come from a low-income family and have always had to fend for yourself. Now you are doing well for yourself and avoid any man who makes less than you or requires financial support from you.

- **Freedom/Autonomy**—your parents suppressed your individual expression or kept you from being you and doing what you truly desired; or you may have suffered from a jealous boyfriend who kept tabs on your every move.

- **Physical touch**—you come from a family that wasn't very familiar with affection or any form of physical contact.

- **Compatible traits and values**—you always tried to "fit in" with your entourage but never found your tribe; people you felt compatible with or with whom you shared values.

Because you suffered from these things in the past, your deal-breakers become non-negotiable for you going into a new relationship. Being aware of these and understanding why they are important to you is another great way to develop eagle-eyed vision (more on this in Chapter 8) and not compromise on them as you start dating. The main thing, though, is to make sure these deal-breakers are clear, to stand true to them, and not to back down on them.

Of course, it's important not to confuse needs with wants and to understand the whys behind our wants. We often think we want certain things, including relationships, but is it really for the right reasons? Answering this is a great way to get to the root of our true desires and assess whether our wants are actually necessary to succeed in building a healthy relationship.

Let me illustrate:

SHANA'S STORY

When I worked with Shana to build her relationship vision, one of the *wants* she had identified regarding her partner was education. It was important that her future man had a high-level education, something like a few university degrees, maybe a PhD.

I asked her why this was important. She explained how her family had always stressed the importance of education and how without it the world wouldn't be very friendly to you. Of course, conditioned by her parents, Shana had several university degrees, including a PhD in electrical engineering. I understood that higher education was a deal-breaker for her. This wasn't a *want*; it was a *need*. It wasn't negotiable.

I asked her, "If you ever met a man that served all the needs you had clearly identified *other than* a university degree or a PhD, would you dismiss him outright?" In more concrete terms, if he instead owned a successful business, was world savvy, intellectual and street smart, would she dismiss him outright just because he didn't have the university title?

Shana paused for quite a while. "I never really considered that," she said.

Through our conversations and the *why* discovery process, Shana finally came to understand that this requirement was not as important to her as it was to her parents. She had been so conditioned to think this was non-negotiable, a deal-breaker. She realized that having a smart/intellectual man was indeed a *need*, but the PhD wasn't. The only reason it was so important to her was because it would make her parents happy. In other words, the *why* behind her *want* for a PhD wasn't the right reason because it wasn't her reason, her own desire, at all. It was important, no doubt, but it wasn't a deal-breaker after all. Shana could have potentially missed many opportunities to meet a great match because of what she was told she *should* want.

Now, this *need* could be moved to the *want* list. It was no longer a deal-breaker. She understood the bigger picture of what really matters. Shana opened up to the possibility of dating someone who fulfilled her needs even without that high-level education.

Discovering the whys behind our wants can be an uncomfortable exercise. It forces us to face our truths and be honest with ourselves for it to work. But this is your life, your relationship. You should never want things just to please other people or accommodate what you've been told by society. You should certainly never want things for the wrong reasons. This will just set you up for failure.

Let's look at this more closely. Say, for example, that you want to be in a relationship because you want a family. For a lot of people, being in a relationship often, eventually, means having kids. But having kids is part of a common goal as a couple, something you go after together. It's certainly not the right reason to want the relationship in the first place.

If you want kids so badly, you could compromise yourself and your needs in the relationship. Even worse, you might not show up as your true authentic self when you meet a potential great guy to father your children.

In a relationship, you need to build and create a foundation first and foremost. Nothing is more important than this, so don't compromise just because you want to have a family. A successful relationship needs a few solid fundamentals with which to build a foundation for future relationships.

Many couples fail at their relationships because they have made it all about the kids. They lose themselves as a couple, and they also lose themselves as individuals. Let's not even mention how that can affect the children when the relationship ends in divorce or, worse, if they continue living together in a toxic, angry environment. Carrying that guilt on your shoulders, on top of the feelings of shame and failing, makes it extremely hard to recover from a divorce.

So, ask yourself *why* you want what you want. Keep yourself rooted in that idea and be sure you're making decisions for the right reasons. Pause now and again to think not only about *why* you want it, but also who you are or who you need to become to get it.

Who do you need to become to get what you want?

Yes, this is a legitimate question. Who do you need to become to receive the vision of the relationship you are looking for? It's easy for us to say what we want and what we need, but are you ready to receive what you truly desire? Have you done all the necessary work to avoid repeating the same patterns or behaviours that had never served you in your past relationships?

It might seem counter-intuitive to suggest we are blocking our own desires, but it happens more often than you can imagine. We end up being our own worst enemy, acting against receiving what we actually want. This is either because we haven't learned from our mistakes or we haven't developed enough self-awareness, which leaves a disconnect between what we think we want and what we really need.

I've worked with many clients that were able to hone their relationship vision to a T. As we continued working through the program, many of them came to realize they didn't feel deserving of a relationship or believe in the possibility it even existed. If you can relate, then you need to work on building your self-worth. How can you attract something you don't believe in or feel worthy of receiving?

So, yes, you have to be clear on what you want, but you also need to be clear on the personal changes you need to make to actually get it. When I was on my own journey to finding love, I created my vision of what I wanted and needed. However, I quickly realized that what I wanted didn't align with who I was.

I wanted to attract a man who was supportive, sensitive, an old-school gentleman, a great communicator, honest, respectful, someone who would appreciate my independence but at the same time take care of me as a woman. However, I was a type-A personality, a control freak, used to managing, organizing, and fixing everything on my own. I was excessively masculine in my energy, not leaving much room for a man to take care of me the way I wanted him to. In other words, I was my own worst enemy.

To attract and be with a supportive man the way I wanted to be, I needed to learn to become softer and gentler in my energy. I needed to practice being vulnerable so my future partner would have room to support and take care of me. I basically needed to allow myself to have a receiving energy.

Oh, boy! A tall order indeed. It really wasn't easy for me to change this way. All of my life I had done it on my own. But, I somehow managed to do it. So can you. You just need to be aware that these changes are not easy because they typically involve going up against years and years of conditioning.

In my case, before meeting my partner I did a lot of small daily exercises to make these changes in my life. These included things like asking my friends and family for help when I needed it, or being open and vulnerable when I was going through tough times instead of keeping it to myself.

Here's the great thing, though; because I had identified these issues beforehand and worked on the changes before I met my man, I was ready to receive him and the vision I had created for myself. Of course, timing is also a very powerful element when you are looking for love, again speaking from personal experience. If I had met Jeff just four months prior, our relationship would never have worked out. Why? Because at that time, I still wasn't ready to receive the kindness he had to offer and especially not how he wanted to provide for me. I would have totally sabotaged myself and kicked him to the curb for being "too nice".

This is not to say it was easy to adjust. But being aware of my past behaviours and patterns and working through them definitely made it easier to receive what I had always wanted and needed from the relationship of my dreams.

So, do yourself a big favour by making a list of what you want and need from your partner and the relationship. Then, ask yourself this: Who do I need to be or become to receive it? Write down all the ideas you can think of and then find ways you can put these into practice in every area of your life, every day.

What do I mean? Let's say, for example, that you are a people pleaser and always do everything for everyone, even at your own expense. You would then need to become less of a giver and more of a receiver. You need to learn to say "no". This can start with co-workers, for example, or with friends. It might even be with your kids. Start practicing these new ways of thinking and behaving in all areas of your life before going into that relationship so that you don't get overwhelmed or retreat to old habits. We typically repeat patterns and actions in the different areas of our life; it's time to change that.

Start doing the work today!

How do you want to feel in your relationship?

Now that you have built a thoroughly clear vision of your relationship, identified your wants, your needs, and who you need to become to get it, let's start working on manifesting it.

Manifesting is drawing something tangible into your life through attraction and belief. The key to attracting something is not only having a clear picture of it in your head, but also feeling it in your heart.

These two components have to be aligned for you to draw something in. In other words, if you can be clear on what you want in your head or on paper, but you don't truly feel it in your heart, the universe won't provide it for you.

When you close your eyes, concentrate on your heart space, not your head. Now, imagine how it feels to be with your partner.

- How does it feel when he kisses you or takes you in his arms?

- How does it feel when he looks you in the eyes?

- How does it feel when you sleep beside each other at night?

- How does it feel when you are dancing or doing a fun physical activity together?

- How does it feel when you are at a party together, each doing your own thing? How connected do you feel?

- How does it feel when you are arguing, or working through your differences?

- How does the idea of sharing your dreams or goals as a couple resonate with you?

Focusing on feelings is a very powerful exercise to also make sure your heart is open to receiving. We don't know how or what the universe will deliver, in what shape it will come in exactly, but we do know the feelings we feel, and these will manifest.

When I used to do my vision exercise, one of the things I'd focus my feelings on was how I'd feel when my future partner would look at me when we'd be at a party, a convention, or any event with a crowd of people. I'd be mingling around, doing my own thing, and he his, but whenever I'd look around to see where he was, to do a check-in, his eyes would naturally meet mine with a smile. There would be that connection.

Today, whenever we're at a party, every single time I look around to see where my man is to make sure he's good, his beautiful blue eyes always meet mine, and every single time my heart melts and I smile because that vision and feeling was realized.

Summary

Be ultra-clear on the reasons behind your wants and if they really matter or not. Being ready to receive what you have clearly created in your vision is key. Ask yourself, "Am I the person I need to be to receive this?" Examine what you need to change in yourself. Also, be clear on your deal-breakers and non-negotiables. This means not compromising as soon as you meet someone that doesn't fit those key criteria you have identified. This will help you stay grounded instead of being blinded by the idea of being in love.

Remember, we want you to have eagle-eyed vision of the big picture.

RAISE YOUR LOVE SIGNAL

Write yourself a letter. Tell yourself how you feel about being in a relationship. Go into as much detail as you can. To do this exercise, I recommend setting the mood. Take a few deep breaths, dim the lights, light some candles, and put on romantic music or anything that inspires you and takes you to your heart space. It's very easy to do this exercise using our minds, but I want you to connect to your heart. I want you to focus on *feeling*. Feeling is a beautiful thing and will help you draw your heart's desire much faster.

LOVE LESSON 2

YOUR SELF

O F THE three Love Lessons in this book, this is the most important one. It's also the hardest to grasp as it demands a lot of self-reflection and a deep discovery to understand the roots of who you are and why you are the way you are. It also aims to reveal why and how you show up, or not, in your relationships.

Understanding where you come from is a key element in your journey to attracting the right partner and being in a healthy relationship. So, buckle up and push through. It might not be easy to get through the coming chapters, but if you do, you will transform yourself and achieve your greatest results.

4

UNDERSTANDING WHERE
YOU COME FROM

I N THIS CHAPTER, we'll start digging into and analyzing your childhood to evaluate the relationships you had with your mother, your father, and the two of them as a couple. This will not only open your eyes to a whole new way of looking at relationships, but it will also give you a new set of tools to help you identify the patterns and behaviours that have frustrated your own ability to succeed in love and to make the necessary changes going forward.

The roots

Our first encounter with love is our parents. I didn't figure this out this until I was thirty-eight! Whether that encounter was good or bad, whether they were present for us or each other or not, the relationships we experienced with our parents or our main caregivers as children are the same ones we end up searching for subconsciously in our own adult relationships. These experiences are also where we pick up our ideas of what love should or should not be. Shocking, isn't it? Can you imagine if we'd been told this earlier in our development?

Our perspectives on how we search for love would be radically different.

The conscious & the subconscious mind

You've heard of the conscious and subconscious mind before, but what does this actually mean? What is the difference between the two of them? In her article, "How to Activate Your Subconscious Mind"[3], Silena Le Beau explains the conscious and subconscious mind as follows: Our **conscious mind** (which accounts for about 10% of our total mind power) deals with logic. It thinks, plans, and analyzes. It stores our short-term memory.

Our **subconscious mind** (accounting for about 90%) is much more complex. It's where we store our long-term memory and our habits, patterns, addictions, and so on. It's where we experience emotions and feelings. It's also the part of our minds that is responsible for our development stages, our spiritual connections, and our creativity and intuition.

Broadly speaking, the conscious mind is responsible for our day-to-day tasks, while most of our significant actions depend on the subconscious mind.

Why is this important to know? It's because our subconscious mind is a powerful tool, but only if we consciously know how to utilize it. When we are born, we are pure, whole, absolutely without judgment in any form. As young children, everything is decided and imposed on us: fears, family values, beliefs, etc., until we are old enough to make our own decisions and develop intellectual independence.

---

3   Le Beau, Silena. "How to Activate Your Subconscious Mind." Vocal. https://vocal. media/longevity/how-to-activate-your-subconscious-mind.

By the time we reach the age of seven, our subconscious minds have already been filled with belief systems that were decided for us. We'll look at beliefs in more detail in Chapter 5, but for now it is vital to understand that this is how our behaviours are created and how we will show up and act in our adult relationships.

This is why it is so important to analyze and reflect on how you were raised. It will shed some serious light on and change your perception of everything you have done so far. Personally, I wish I had known all this much sooner. It would've helped me break my patterns much more quickly instead of letting these patterns feed my self-doubt. At the very least, it would have enabled me to understand why certain scenarios kept recurring in my life, including the kinds of men I was attracting.

Anyway, I really wish all parents would learn this before having children so that they don't project their own fears and belief systems onto their children who haven't yet experienced the idiosyncrasies of life. This is how family patterns repeat, from one generation to the next. It's time to break this cycle.

Digging into your childhood

Let me share with you, as an example, my own experiences with my mother, my father, their relationship, and the family values I was raised with.

Relationship with my father

All my life, I kept attracting emotionally unavailable men. I was really good with long distance relationships, dating much younger men, and attracting already involved men.

I couldn't understand why this kept happening. No matter what I tried, I just couldn't seem to break this pattern. Until one day, just before I turned forty, I decided to explore a very deep form of therapy. Through this work, I finally understood why this had been the case. You see, my father died suddenly in a car crash when I was just two years old.

According to my mom, I was daddy's little girl, madly in love with the first man I had ever laid eyes on. We had a very strong bond. Needless to say, when he suddenly never came back home again, that little two-year-old girl registered feelings of abandonment and rejection.

From that day on, my subconscious mind had taken note: "Men will leave you when you love them. They are not reliable. I will never let a man hurt me that way ever again."

I finally understood that attracting emotionally unavailable men was a protective mechanism for me. I knew deep down that these relationships wouldn't last and it was a way for me to stay in control of the situation. However, these kinds of relationships consistently made me feel unworthy and unvalued. They also made me compromise my identity and personal values most of the time. I lacked love for myself, so I was always looking for it as an outside source of validation. How could I then possibly attract the right guy?

Relationship with my mother

When my father passed away, he left not only me, but also my mom and my six-month-old brother. My parents were young and just starting out in life, with a very low income to survive. Suddenly, here was a single mother of two babies, who had just lost the love of her life, having to learn overnight how to juggle the demands of working to support her family and of raising kids, alone.

Growing up, as I was the older sister, I subconsciously took on the role of an adult. I felt I had to protect my mother and brother. I still remember when my mom would go out on a date (which was so very rare), I would tell her what to wear. If she ever eventually chose to present a man to us, I became a protective pit-bull, just like any father looking out for his daughter. I laugh about it now, but I really did not make it easy for these men.

Fast-forward to adulthood... I became a control freak, a highly independent woman, a go-getter with a great ability to organize and manage just about anything. I needed to survive. I rationalized that if I didn't take care of me, no one else would.

Now, you might say, "Chantal, these are great qualities to have," and I would reply, "Yeah, absolutely!" I wouldn't have gotten where I am today without them. However, every great quality can also become a debilitating fault, and vice versa.

In my case, my control issues killed most of my relationships, even with friends and co-workers, because as soon as things weren't going my way, I'd become a nagging bitch, with a nasty attitude and just all-around not very nice. Men would often view my independence as me being the cool girl, "one of the boys". But this didn't leave them much room for the hunt or for me to be desired, which further disconnected me from my feminine energy. I had built a wall of stone around my heart. Let me tell you, it's pretty hard to bring love into your heart through a stone wall.

Relationship with my parents as a couple

Since my father had passed away, I didn't get to experience seeing my parents being in their relationship. Instead, I was exposed to my mother playing both parenting roles, which is why my masculine energy[4] took such a strong hold.

Added to this, my mom was always careful and selective about whom she would introduce her kids to. I can only recount three of them as being meaningful and present, including the first man she dated after my father's passing. What I got to observe then was a woman very submissive to her man, and fragile, vulnerable, desiring to be loved.

It's no wonder I adopted that same desperation and desire to be loved in my adult life. I can't tell you how many times I cried myself to sleep over the years thinking I wasn't worthy of love and that I would never find or experience love the way my heart so desperately wanted to feel it. It makes me so sad when I think about those moments today. No child should have to deal with these kinds of thoughts.

Family values

My mother was raised in a very dysfunctional family. She was the oldest of five kids in a fairly low-income family, with both parents being alcoholics and not very good at communicating or showing any form of emotion. She had to work for

---

4   Masculine and feminine energies represent two powerful forces that exist within all of us regardless of gender. Having an awareness of both energies' strengths and weaknesses is essential to balancing them in your relationship.

Masculine energy is often associated with qualities like strength, assertiveness, and rationality. It exudes a remarkable strength in problem-solving, getting things done, setting boundaries, and taking decisive action. As a fault, it can manifest as stubbornness, emotional detachment, impatience, and difficulty receiving.

Feminine energy is linked to qualities such as intuition, empathy, and being nurturing. It excels in creating emotional connections, support, and playfulness. As a fault, it suggests being susceptible, indecisive, and overly emotional. It also has a tendency to prioritize others' needs over one's own.

everything she earned, be responsible for her siblings, and contribute to the family's income. In other words, she had to be an adult from a very young age.

It's not a stretch to say these types of behaviours and beliefs can be passed on from generation to generation. My mother raised us to be very independent, with a strong work ethic. She believed that if we worked hard, we would be able to achieve anything we wanted and not have to rely on anyone but ourselves to get anything done. She also taught us the value of money, particularly how to be frugal because money never comes easy. Being affectionate and having open communication was another value she emphasized, because she missed it. In other words, she took a completely opposite approach to parenting than she had experienced herself.

Consequently, her behaviours and beliefs became ours, her values became ours. These have stuck with me and apply to every area of my life. I believe I can do or become anything I want if I work for it. I have learned to develop great communication skills and to be extremely affectionate with those close to me and whom I cherish. Sounds awesome, right?

Well, here's the flipside. Until recently, I noticed I still had a huge hang-up about money and its accessibility because I had always been told it was limited. (My mom still drives this idea home to this day!) Even when I finally reached some financial stability, I struggled to allow myself to spend money because of that deep-seated belief I had absorbed. I'd keep having these kinds of conversations in my head: "What if it runs out? I don't have anyone to support me. I can't justify this. I don't deserve to spend this kind of money," and so on.

Do you see the dots connecting here? Our childhood experiences form both our adulthood wounds and our desires. We are an accumulation of reactions to the traumas we have experienced since childhood. And the trauma doesn't even have to be terribly traumatic; what matters is the way we reacted to the world around us that created these imprints on us.

Attachment styles

To better understand these imprints, let's look into attachment styles. In 2020, I read a book called *Attached*, by Amir Levine and Rachel Heller. It was a game changer for me. It really helped me understand my relationships and shift my perspectives on them.

According to this book, "attachment styles" describe the ways we attract who we do and why we behave the way we do in our relationships based on our childhood interactions with our primary caregivers. As we saw earlier in this chapter, recognizing our childhood root sources really helps us understand why we repeatedly end up in the same situations, even if this happens with different partners.

The original idea of attachment styles was introduced in the 1950s by John Bowlby, a psychiatrist and psychoanalyst, who developed Attachment Theory. This theory posits that "one's relationship with his/her parents during childhood has an overarching influence on the person's social and intimate relationships and even relationships at work in the future." Amazing, isn't it? What's even more amazing is that this can begin happening as early as two years old. Just practically a baby and already your belief system and future relationship patterns are being set for you, with no control or choice on your part.

Yet, it can be changed. One way to do this is by doing the kind of work we're doing now, together. Ideally, if you plan on having children, you should do this work prior so that you are aware of the influence you have as a parent. At the very minimum, this should happen as a young adult to avoid spending most of one's life, as I had, not understanding how we show up in relationships.

This is exactly why I do what I do: talk to and coach women about all these different aspects of ourselves. Knowing these ideas can literally decide your life path in all of your relationships. How different would your life be now if you had been made aware of all this stuff at a younger age? It's possible you might have saved yourself from many toxic relationships, or even just disappointing and failed connections.

The three main attachment styles

Attached outlines three main attachment styles: Secure, Anxious, and Avoidant.

Let's look at each and describe how they develop in childhood and end up affecting your behaviour in relationships later on.

Secure

This attachment style develops if you grew up in a space where you felt safe, listened to, accepted for your uniqueness. Your primary caregivers demonstrated affection and support. You felt loved.

In a relationship, Secure types feel comfortable expressing emotions openly. Their relationships are based on honesty, tolerance, and emotional closeness. They can rely on their partner and vice versa without the fear of being alone. They have a very positive view of themselves and others.

Anxious

This attachment style develops if you grew up not knowing if your primary caregivers would show up for you and provide any form of affection. They would be distant. You just couldn't rely on any form of stability or feelings of safety.

In a relationship, Anxious types typically develop a strong fear of abandonment, so individuals require a lot of attention and care from their partners. The absence of support and intimacy can lead the anxious to become clingy and demanding. They seek approval and support from their partner. Their partner is often considered their "better half".

Avoidant

This attachment style develops if people grew up with inconsistent caregivers. They didn't know if they would show up or not, and when they did, it was unpredictable if they would be affectionate or distant. This style doesn't offer space for any of your emotional needs, only the physiological ones.

In relationships, Avoidants perceive themselves as the "lone soldier"—independent, self-sufficient, and strong. They don't like depending on others or have others depending on them. They typically hide or suppress their feelings when faced with emotional conflicts. They tend to believe they don't have to be in a relationship to feel complete.

Remember: Attachment styles don't define you. They can change and evolve if you work on yourself. I transformed from being a very Avoidant type for most of my life to the Secure type I am now.

Getting familiar with this concept will undoubtedly help you identify how you relate to others, both personally and professionally. It will also help you identify with whom you connect and why you choose the partners you do.

The quickest way to overcome difficult emotions is to build the courage to go straight at them. In the meantime, if you want to know more details, I strongly recommend reading *Attached*.

DEAN'S STORY

Dean lived with an Anxious attachment style, displaying a fear of abandonment and seeking reassurance from his partner, Sarah. Hers was an Avoidant attachment style, showing discomfort with closeness and a preference for independence.

Dean's Anxious attachment triggered Sarah's Avoidant tendencies, leading her to withdraw emotionally and physically. Dean's clingy behaviour and constant need for reassurance further fueled Sarah's Avoidant behaviours, resulting in a cycle of insecurity and distance in their relationship. Through therapy, and getting familiar with the attachment style theory, Dean learned to manage his anxiety and communicate his needs effectively, while Sarah developed trust in their relationship.

Over time, their relationship improved as they each developed a more Secure attachment style. This shows the significant impact of attachment styles on romantic relationships and the potential for positive change through knowledge, self-awareness, and communication.

Summary

Dig into your childhood. Take the time to evaluate the relationships you had with each of your parents as individuals, and also consider how they were together as a couple. You should notice relatively quickly why you act the way you do as well as where your recurring patterns come from. Identifying the family values you were raised with will likewise help you understand why you search for certain qualities in your partners, as well as why you act and show up in your relationships the way you do. Get familiar with the concept of attachment styles and use it as a tool to develop an awareness of patterns that don't work for you in relationships. This is the only way you be able to reprogram and rewire your brain.

RAISE YOUR LOVE SIGNAL

Create an inventory of the family beliefs and limitations you inherited from your father, your mother, and from your parents as a couple.

Take the Attachment style quiz by visiting https://attachment.personaldevelopmentschool.com/quiz.

Become familiar with your own attachment style. Reflect on the main characteristics of each as they relate to you. Try identifying your close friends' styles. This will open your eyes to new possibilities and realities, and it will help you better understand how people show up for you and you for them. Committing yourself to this practice will provide you with another tool to help you develop that eagle-eyed vision during dating.

5

IDENTIFYING
LIMITING BELIEFS

S O FAR, by looking at your family roots we have figured out where you're coming from, your formative influences, and why you act the way you do. Now, let's start to focus on the limiting beliefs you've developed throughout your childhood and even early adulthood.

Limiting beliefs are thoughts, core beliefs, emotions, and behaviours that we take as the absolute truth. They are stories we have created from childhood that we tell ourselves over and over again, thereby making them part of our identity. These stories end up holding us back from our own success.

Some of you may know this as that negative chatter in the back of your mind, something that can sound a little like this:

- I am not good enough.
- I'm too old to start a new career.
- What will everyone think?
- No one will ever love me the way I am.
- I'm not good in relationships.
- I'm not knowledgeable enough.
- I don't have enough money to take this course, do that therapy, hire the necessary help, and so on.

Our brains love to be right. So, often repeated, our words become our reality. As a result, we feel a strong need to identify with them, even if they stop us from taking action, even if we know they are not helping us. Why? Because we love to play it safe. We are our own worst enemies and end up not living our true authentic lives.

Limiting beliefs get in the way

Limiting beliefs can show up in different areas of our lives and get in the way of us living it. Let me give you an example.

Being raised by a single mother on a low income, I didn't get an allowance like other kids. I started working at fourteen to be able to have my own money to go out with my friends or buy myself some clothes I really liked—in other words, anything "extra" my mom couldn't afford. At seventeen, I decided to move from Ottawa to Montreal to study theater. I knew my mom could barely make ends meet, let alone pay for my tuition or apartment. So, I moved in with a roommate and found an almost full-time job to support myself. It was just the way it was. Given the situation, it was really hard for me to ask for help. My pride and ego rules my world, shouting, "I got this! I am strong, I am independent. I can do it!" One of the core beliefs I had registered in my subconscious mind by then was that *to get anything I want in life, I have to do it on my own.*

Do you know how hard it is to do and accomplish everything alone, all the time? Sure, I managed to do anything I set my mind to, but that doesn't mean it came without struggles. There were many lonely nights of crying myself to sleep, thinking "Why do I have to do everything alone? Can't I just be taken care of for once in my life?"

You can't imagine how this thinking weighed down on me all my life. That is, until I eventually learned about my belief systems, identified their roots, and finally rewired my brain from *I have to do everything by myself to accomplish anything*, to *I don't need to do and accomplish everything on my own*.

Learning to ask for help was one thing, but then learning to receive and accept it was a whole other. Today, I am proud to say it is easier for me to ask for help and/or support when I need it because I also learned how to accept to receive help when it is offered. I was able to overcome this major limiting belief.

We humans hate change. Change is never easy, and we fight against it all the time. I won't lie; it was not at all simple to change my way of thinking that had persisted for forty years. When I finally realized how these deep-seated beliefs kept me from attracting the relationship vision I had created for myself, I knew I needed to do something to reprogram my thinking. It's crucial to keep in mind that change does not happen overnight; it takes time, effort, and patience. As I mentioned earlier in the book, you need to start incorporating small changes, new patterns in all areas of your life to make bigger changes happen over time. These daily fixes will transform the mental processes impacting your limiting beliefs. I started with basic things like asking for help lifting a heavy box, or asking a friend to listen when things weren't going my way with someone I was dating. I put myself out there, allowed myself to be vulnerable in every area of my life until I eventually developed new muscles (figuratively speaking). I accepted that I don't have to do everything on my own.

Baby steps

The good news is that once you've identified what your root beliefs are, you have accomplished 50% of the work. That's because you now have awareness. It's easier to work through issues when we've identified the problem, right?

The average person goes through life without ever questioning themselves when the same things happen over and over again. Still, today, I have moments when it's hard for me to receive or ask for help. But, because I am aware of these issues, it's easier to talk myself out of falling into those old patterns again. I have even gone so far as to name my subconscious mind "Little C". And when Little C comes out with her old habits, "Chantal", the conscious me, will call her out on it and say, "No, no, no, no! You don't own me anymore. That was the old me. I am no longer that person anymore." It's like I'm talking to my six-year-old self who got caught doing something naughty and tries to deny it. But, you know what? It works every time.

So, now, after you've identified your beliefs and developed an awareness of them, the next step is to incorporate these practices in every area of your life, not just in your relationships. The more you practice those different thoughts and actions before you find your partner, the easier it will be when you are in the actual relationship. For the time being, it's all about taking baby steps to change.

In my own case, I started applying my changes by asking co-workers for help when I needed it. I also approached a very close friend, whom I completely trust, and made a pact with her to be vulnerable and share my feelings when I was going through something difficult instead of keeping it to myself. That one friend led to a second ear, and then a third. Today, I am much more open about sharing my feelings with just about anyone I feel comfortable with when I'm going through stuff. I am especially great at it with my man when dealing with our relationship. Those daily baby steps really helped to rewire those old, rooted ways of thinking.

Let me tell you, life is so much better knowing I don't have to live as a solo warrior fighting battles. Everything in life is better when you feel supported and learn to receive the help your loved ones are willing to give you. I don't cry myself to sleep anymore out of loneliness, or from having to do everything alone, because I built a community and I allow myself to receive what it offers.

But, don't just take my word for it.

EMILIA'S STORY

Emilia worked intensely and meticulously to get a clear vision of her partner and the relationship she wanted to attract. Everything was detailed and thought through. I even sensed the emotion behind it. It was like reading a romance novel.

"Wow!" I said to her. "How does it make you feel knowing this is what you are calling into your life to receive?"

She started crying.

"Emilia, why are you crying?"

"Because I just realized I don't feel deserving of it."

"Why is that?" I asked.

"I need to lose weight before I can attract a man like that. Who is going to love chubby me?"

Since childhood, Emilia, unlike her sister, had had an issue with her weight. She grew up constantly comparing herself to her sister and ended up creating a story in her head that to be loved she needed to be skinny.

"I am not worthy of love until I lose weight," was her belief system.

Being skinny is not what makes you worthy of love. But Emilia's subconscious mind had decided that it was. She hadn't realized she had this hidden belief until we worked on her beliefs together. Until you are able to identify your belief systems, you could be spinning tales and repeating the same mistakes over and over. Emilia had been self-sabotaging all her life, not allowing herself to receive love. Once she finally identified the beliefs that needed to be reprogrammed, she was able to attract the high-quality man she had envisioned and has since built a healthy relationship with him.

Emilia started putting her daily self-love rituals into practice to take ownership of who she was so she could learn to love and accept herself 100%, no matter her weight.

Understanding past behaviours

Other by-products of our belief systems (I told you this Love Lesson wasn't going to be easy…) are behaviours that are meant to either protect us or make us feel safe, or thoughts that are simply there to rationalize our belief systems in the first place.

Because these beliefs stay with us, all of their associated behaviours do, too, and they will show up in our relationships. It is crucial, then, to identify those behaviours that haven't served you in your past failed relationships so you can eliminate them, or at least be aware of them when they come up.

Earlier, I mentioned a belief from my childhood, the one that goes like "To get anything I want in life, I need to do it alone." This showed up in my relationships as a total lack of vulnerability, especially hiding emotions during hardships or tough days. I never asked for help or relied on anyone, and, even worse, I had to control everything, including the relationship.

That is so unhealthy!

Going forward, I needed to become more vulnerable, to let go of control, to become a better communicator. Once I pinpointed these needs, I had to take steps to put these ideas into practice.

When I work with clients, I have them list their behavioural patterns that haven't serviced them in any way in past relationships and then ask them to link these to new behaviours they need to integrate as replacements. After all, only you can do this, to start attracting different and healthy relationships.

I'll say it again . . . *you* are responsible for creating change within yourself.

Healing past wounds

I honestly believe that wounds shape us, but they don't define us. Unless we let them. Not healing our past wounds can prevent us from going forward, it can keep us miserable, or worse, it can make us carry extra weight into our new relationship that is not our partner's to bear. That said, pain is an incredible teacher if you choose to understand the lessons it offers, and when we do learn these lessons we typically don't repeat them. The key is not to feel any shame about them or let them control us; instead, we must learn to use the pain to grow and evolve.

Towards that end, ask yourself questions like "What did I learn about myself? If the same thing were to happen again, how could I do it differently? What are the changes I need to apply?"

I heard this expression somewhere (wish I could remember where) and I think it perfectly encapsulates what I'm trying to say: "post-traumatic wisdom". If you choose to grow and evolve from your wounds instead of staying stuck in them, hurt and victimized, the wisdom you accumulate thereby is as good as gold.

Identifying wounds you've experienced throughout your life can have a significant impact on you. Once you've done this, ask yourself if these wounds are still open. Have you made peace with all of them? Are there still open wounds that could be keeping you from having the love and the life you wish for?

Consider this example: If you were cheated on in your last relationship or in multiple relationships, you have most likely developed a serious problem with trust, right? It makes perfect sense that you would. Unhealed, you could potentially go into a new relationship guarded, skeptical, and untrusting of this new person. You would walk into that new relationship with a brick wall around your heart (to protect it), though you might be thinking your heart is open. The problem is that you wouldn't be able to show any form of vulnerability.

You'd feel insecure or jealous anytime your new man is in the presence of a woman in any given situation. You might even start developing toxic behaviours such as checking his phone, or eavesdropping on his conversations. Does this sound fun to you? It doesn't sound very healthy, does it? And, it's certainly not at all fair to this new guy.

Here's an exercise: Write down all the past wounds you have experienced. Use the pain as a source of meaning... What is it telling you? Have the wounds healed? Are you noticing any recurring wounds from one relationship to the next?

Bringing unresolved baggage into your next relationship and making your partner pay for it won't lead to a healthy relationship. Recognize what is no longer of service; you may just discover a pattern that needs to be broken. Be gentle on yourself and learn to laugh. That is paramount.

Being aware is half the battle. Change your triggers, change your life!

Summary

Take the time to recognize your limiting beliefs. This will help you identify the changes you need to make to rewire your brain. Start incorporating these changes in baby steps in every area of your life. Keep in mind that deep-seated beliefs, which have been there for most of our lives, do not disappear with a snap of a finger. You need to work every day to remove those old habits.

You also need to pinpoint behaviours that hadn't worked for you in past relationships to avoid repeating them. Ask yourself instead who you need to become so that you can go forward. Doing this will set you up for success and help you show up in a whole new way when you find your right partner.

Lastly, make sure you start that relationship with a clean slate. Don't carry unhealed wounds that your new loved one will potentially have to pay for.

RAISE YOUR LOVE SIGNAL

1   In your journal, write down six behaviours that hadn't worked for you or that prevented the success of your past relationships. Once you have identified them, write down who you need to become in your next relationship to make sure you don't repeat the same mistakes. For example:

- If you were always a giver in a relationship...

    - Giver now needs *to become* a receiver.

- If you were a people pleaser and compromised yourself...

    - You need *to become* better at stating your boundaries and stay true to who you are.

2   Identify the wounds you experienced through the course of your life that had an impact on you. Ask yourself: Are they healed? If not, what work do I need to do, or help I need to get to overcome them?

6

SELF-LOVE

THIS ONE'S a biggie! And probably the hardest lesson of all. In this chapter, we'll look at the practice of self-love and understanding your worth. We will also talk about the importance of setting boundaries and how doing so ensures you stay true to who you are and don't lose yourself in your new relationship.

Understanding self-love

So, what exactly is self-love? In a nutshell, it means that you accept yourself fully, treat yourself with kindness and respect, and nurture your growth and well-being.

Now, you might be thinking, "Chantal, what are you talking about? I love me."

I can guarantee you that every single one of us has been guilty of not practicing self-love at some point. Consider:

- All the mothers out there who put everyone else ahead of themselves

- All the women suffering from unresolved traumas, pains, and failed relationships

- All the women comparing themselves: I'm not as young, as pretty, as skinny, as smart as . . . I am not doing as much, as well, as . . ., etc.

- All the teenagers and young women trying to figure out who they are and have no idea what self-love means

I am sure most of us can identify with at least one of these examples. The problem is that we've just never been taught anything about it, including how to deal with it. In fact, you'd be surprised how often this surfaces in my sessions with clients. They are desperately looking for love, thinking they are ready for it, but as we go through the phases of the program they realize they are struggling with loving themselves or don't feel worthy of it.

The benefits of practicing self-love show up in many different ways:

- It allows us to be assertive, set boundaries, and prevent others from taking advantage of us.

- It allows us to create healthy relationships with others, practice self-care, pursue our interests and goals, and feel proud of who we are.

- Loving ourselves first allows us to say "no", to ask for help, and not to feel guilty for putting our needs first.

- It allows us to reject things or situations we typically wouldn't accept, to be kind to ourselves in hard times, to refuse crumbs from the men we date.

- It allows us to value our own feelings, recognize our own strengths, and accept our flaws and imperfections.

- It allows us to notice and appreciate our progress and efforts.

I could go on and on, but this should give you an idea. Start incorporating a self-love exercise into your daily routine. This can be anything from a positive and self-supportive thought to an outright action.

All this is based on the idea that before you even think of being in a relationship, you need to learn to accept that you deserve the relationship, the love, and to be loved. As I mentioned earlier, many of my clients think they are ready for love but, deep down, believe they are unworthy of it. They struggle to love themselves first. If you experience this type of inner chatter and don't address it, the process of attracting a high-quality partner, of finding your soulmate, will be much more difficult.

And, hey, none of us are perfect. But you know what? We are perfectly us. **You are perfectly you.** There is just one *you* on this planet. Take the time to embrace all of you, good and bad. Make this the game changer in terms of the quality of the relationships you attract.

Also, remember you're not alone on this path. Self-love was a huge part of my own journey to where I am today, that is, in a healthy relationship with myself and with my partner. To be fair, most people I met had taken me for a confident person. At least, on the outside. But inside? Wow, was I ever lacking self-love and self-worth. (I'll dive deeper into self-worth a little later in this chapter.)

I want to share with you a few things I've learned over the years to help me develop a very healthy self-love practice routine.

Self-love exercises

Affirmations

A great way to start loving you, all of you, is with affirmation practice. I love affirmations and I still apply them daily.

Affirmations are powerful. When done properly, they can help rewire your thoughts, either to eliminate something from your life or to help bring something new into it. It tells your subconscious mind, "I am aware that there is something I can do to change this." To be fair, every thought we think and every word we speak is an affirmation. We are always applying affirmations without even knowing it.

Think about your regular inner chatter, for example. Every time you complain about something, or think about something you don't want, it's an affirmation. So, when you get angry or feel like a victim, you are actually affirming to your subconscious mind that you want to feel more of that. Whenever life isn't giving you what you want, pay close attention to the conversation you hold with yourself.

The same works in reverse. The more you choose to think thoughts that make you feel good, the quicker your affirmations will work in a positive way. Of course, you have to be consistent in your practice and make sure to focus on how the affirmation makes you feel. And it's not just the thought of it in your mind ... you really need to believe it to feel it. This is a key component: *feel*, don't *think* (exactly as I explained in Chapter 3). It's easy to put words together and say them out loud, but it needs to come from the heart space. You have to have your brain and your heart aligned.

Start this exercise by finding two or three affirmations that resonate with you. Repeat them as a mantra when you first wake up in the morning and before you go to bed at night. I often repeat my affirmations throughout the day, depending on what I am trying to call into my life. But again, don't treat this like a to-do list. Feel it, empower these thoughts and feelings, let the vibrations of these words fill you.

Self-reliant happiness

"I will be happy when I meet the partner of my dreams, when I lose weight, when I make X amount of money, when I get my promotion, when I have kids, when I have that car…"

Sound familiar?

It's easy to rely on outside sources, the idea of having this or that, for our happiness as opposed to learning to cultivate it within ourselves. But happiness is not a destination. It's a state of being.

For the longest time, my BFF and I dreamt of going to Santorini, Greece. We dreamt about making the trip with our respective partners. "When we find our guy…" By the time she was about to hit forty, we were both still single with absolutely no prospects on the horizon. "Will this ever happen for us?" Then one day, she said, "Chantal, what about doing this trip together for my fortieth? If we keep waiting for love to do this trip, who knows when it will happen."

"Let's do it," I said.

We planned the exact trip we had fantasized we'd do with our future partners, and then did it. To this day, my trip to Greece with Tina was one of the best experiences either of us have ever had. We never imagined we could have such a beautiful time having previously limited ourselves to thinking it had to be with our "partners".

The moral of the story? Don't wait for or rely on outside sources to create your happiness. Make your own, now!

Gratitude practice

Oprah Winfrey introduced me to the concept of gratitude practice in her article "What Oprah Knows for Sure About Gratitude"[5]. I knew nothing about this idea until I heard her explain the philosophy behind it. "Focus on the good you have in life, the joy of simple moments," she said. It caught my attention. The idea of being thankful for the little things we easily take for granted resonated with me. Within days, I developed a habit of jotting down what I was grateful for and I kept this up on a weekly basis. I soon noticed a clear shift in my attitude and how my appreciation for the little things was changing. I eventually graduated to doing this daily. I discovered the five-minute gratitude journal—every morning, before I start my day, I write down three things I am grateful for. Every evening, before I go to bed, I write down three things I am grateful for that happened through the day.

It really helps put things into perspective and to focus on the positives, especially when I've had a rough day. Because even on those days, there is always something to be grateful for. Otherwise, it can be really easy to focus on what we don't have, as opposed to remembering what we do.

Don't limit your gratitude practice to yourself. Be social about it with your friends, your kids, even co-workers. I've even convinced my beau to take up this practice. On weekends, when we have our pillow talk or connect over coffee, we share what we are grateful for with each other.

---

5   Winfrey, Oprah. "Oprah's Gratitude Journal: Oprah on Gratitude." Oprah.com. https://www.oprah.com/spirit/oprahs-gratitude-journal-oprah-on-gratitude.

My lesson with self-love and self-worth

I spent most of my life thinking I was never enough, and I wasn't even aware I was doing it. This showed in the quality of my relationships and even in those I didn't have because I missed out on them. I didn't accept self-love until I turned forty-four years old. That's crazy!

Now that I think back on it, I always doubted my bubbly personality and witty charm because I had convinced myself I wasn't pretty enough compared to my group of women friends. Of course, making my looks such an important factor was simply not healthy. But, the real underlying factor was that I didn't feel worthy of love. My looks had absolutely nothing to do with it.

This was my inner chatter: "This guy can't be interested in a girl like me." Or "I'm not good enough for a guy like that." I constantly made these decisions for men. It was my protection mechanism, which had developed into self-sabotage to avoid the situation (totally Avoidant attachment style).

I finally found my self-worth after a very brief dating episode with a man. At the time, I was just getting over another short-lived love story with a man I thought was "my one". As it turned out, that story, like many others before it, ended abruptly and left me disappointed, hurt, and disillusioned about love. I was crushed and felt so sorry for myself that I didn't leave my home for a couple of weeks.

One night, I remember it like it was yesterday, a friend of mine invited me to a fancy restaurant opening. I hesitated at first, but then I told myself, "Enough, Chantal. Time to get yourself out of this funk. You are going to dress up, go out, and talk to every single person who has something interesting to share." I did just that. I put on a beautiful dress, curled my hair, and painted my lips red. I was ready to socialize and have some fun. Finally!

One thing I decided to work on was to expand the range of men I "thought" were my type. We tend to be very narrow-minded when it comes to our type, and I was certainly not an exception to the rule. That night I proved to myself I was on the right path.

Because I was open to meeting *anyone*, not just who I thought was my type, I ended up meeting three great guys that I wouldn't have typically been attracted to. I had three very meaningful interactions and conversations.

One gentleman in particular managed to really make an impression. He had a British accent and was very witty and intellectual. I was intrigued. We ended up exchanging numbers and meeting for drinks the following week. We connected on a deep emotional intelligence level; our conversations were meaningful and focused on life and philosophy. We were both in awe of how refreshing it was to have such a connection on this level.

However, he was just coming out of a painful divorce after many years of marriage because his wife had been suffering from mental health issues. He was dealing with a lot of guilt for having ultimately left her. Needless to say, he wasn't quite ready to begin a new relationship. He had healing to do.

I remember feeling frustrated and thinking, "Why is this happening to me, again? Why am I attracting an emotionally unavailable man after all the work I had done on myself over the last couple of years?" I was so angry at the universe, but something about him kept me going back.

In one of our many discussions, he questioned why I was still single. At this point, he had gotten to know my way of thinking, my value system, and everything I had to bring to the table not only as a woman but also as a partner in a relationship.

Then came the magical words that would forever change my life:

"Chantal, I don't think you see or know your own worth. You have been fishing at the bottom of the sea, not the top."

"What do you mean?" I asked, feeling puzzled.

"When you fish at the bottom of the sea, you eat all the shit left from the fish on top. Do you want to be with a bottom feeder or with the high-quality fish that swim at the top of the ocean?"

Was that ever an Ah-ha moment for me! He was completely right. I didn't see my own value or believe I could attract a high-quality man. From that day forward, my eyes opened to a whole new perspective of myself and I stepped into my worth like never before. I started allowing myself to believe that the kind of man and relationship I wanted was possible for me.

In fact, I ended our encounter very shortly after because I knew he wasn't able to give me what I was looking for. Sticking around would have made me a bottom feeder again. This was a major act of self-love and self-worth.

I never looked back. And I will never, ever regret that encounter. He gave me the missing piece to complete my self-love/worth puzzle and opened me to receive the relationship I am in today.

Life has a funny way of putting the right people on your path, but only if you choose to see them that way and pay attention to the lessons they offer. (Remember what I said in Chapter 5 about healing your wounds?)

So, now, ask yourself this: Do you know your self-worth? Do you feel worthy of love?

If you answered no to either of these questions, then **the person keeping you from attracting the relationship of your dreams might just be you.**

Self-acceptance

Accepting who you are is also a part of your self-love journey. After all, if you don't accept who you are whole-heartedly, how do you expect to be loved by another in a healthy way?

Learn to see yourself as you are, with your flaws and your strengths, without fear or judgment. Always remember, the end goal is to be loved for the true you— the whole of you, not the accommodating person you are pretending to be. After all, your partner can only love you as much as you love yourself.

Read Emilia's story again; do you recall how she felt she needed to be skinny to be worthy of love? The first thing Emilia needed to do was work on her own self-love/worth. She needed to accept her body. Emilia was a gorgeous, intelligent, and vibrant woman full of life, but she was also her own worst enemy. Once she started practicing her exercises, including affirmations, to change her negative thought patterns and remind herself daily of all of the amazing qualities she had, she managed to rewire her brain and to embrace and accept herself. You can, too.

Setting boundaries

It is one thing to really be you, but making sure you are accepted and respected for all of you is another. Setting healthy boundaries is a way to protect and care for what matters to us and to control who enters our psychological and physical space. When you learn to clearly express your boundaries, and stay true to them, you also honour your self-worth. This is a huge part of self-care, primarily as it prevents you from losing your individuality while simultaneously empowering you to make better choices. Learning this will also help you maintain healthy relationships in every area of your life, be they at work or with family, your kids, or friends. It's important to set them, keep them, and not settle for anyone who doesn't respect them.

This all ties in together: setting boundaries + self-love = self-worth and higher-quality relationships.

In Love Lesson #1, we covered the importance of being clear on your needs in a relationship. This clarity will help you identify your boundaries and make sure you don't compromise them when you start dating. The clearer you are about them, the more you will stay focused on what really matters, not get lost in the shiny new object syndrome, and not excuse unwanted behaviours from your new partner.

Here are a few questions you can ask yourself to see if you are struggling with setting boundaries:

- Do you avoid speaking up for yourself?

- Do you let bad situations go without reacting to them?

- Do you tend to avoid conflict or let others make decisions for you?

- Do you doubt your right to have your needs met?

- Do you often agree to do things you really don't want to do and hate yourself for it later?

If you've answered "yes" to most of these questions, it's time to stand up for yourself, speak your truth, and set your boundaries. Start by taking the time to identify your needs and the boundaries you struggle to share or affirm. Then, identify how you can assert them in every area of your life. As with the limiting beliefs and the practice of rewiring your brain, this starts with baby steps.

Let's say, for example, you struggle with saying "no" to demands or events you don't want to do or attend. In what area of your life does this happen? How can you start incorporating change? This might be with a co-worker that takes advantage of you when they need something, or it might be as simple as your kids asking you for dessert before they finish their meals.

Pick one area, and set your boundary. Then, say "no" when the situation doesn't work for you.

Repeat.

One of my boundaries

Jeff, my partner, is always late. That's just his nature, and a well-known fact about him among his friends and co-workers. It drives me crazy. I am extremely punctual. Being late, in my mind, is a sign of disrespect. Needless to say, this has caused a lot of friction between us.

I had to set a boundary with him. He can be late any time he wants, except when it involves me. I understand that I can't control what he does outside of our time together, but he can make it a point to plan accordingly to make sure he honours and respects my boundary.

On a side note, remember that once you set your boundaries and expect your partner to respect and honour them, you need to reciprocate and adjust to your partner's boundaries. In fact, this should be the case in all of your relationships. Since Jeff and I each set our boundaries and learned to honour and respect them, it's worked very well for us.

Summary

To be in a healthy relationship, you need to love yourself first. This can show up in many different ways, but the key element is making sure you fully accept yourself and treat yourself with kindness. Start integrating the tips I've shared on how to develop a regular self-love practice. Also, remember that feeling worthy of love and knowing your worth are a mindset you should not doubt. Finally, learning to set healthy boundaries is important to maintain balanced relationships. It's a great way to make sure you do not compromise your needs or tolerate unwanted things in the long term.

RAISE YOUR LOVE SIGNAL

In your journal, try to answer these questions: "Do I feel worthy of the love and the relationship I desire?" If not, ask yourself, "Why not? What is stopping or blocking me from receiving it?"

Also, start practicing affirmations out loud, or at least repeat them silently over and over in your head so they can help rewire your brain. Find three to five that work for you and repeat them daily. Here are some great examples:

- It is safe for me to love and be loved.

- I am beautiful inside and out.

- I let go of that which no longer serves me.

- I am kind and compassionate with myself whom I love, appreciate, and respect.

- I believe in myself.

- I am loved and lovable.

- Everything I need is within me. I love and cherish my body.

Gratitude practice: Learn to say thank you for everything. It's simple, but it creates a huge shift. Even better, get yourself a gratitude journal, such as *The 5-minute Journal* or *The Gratitude Journal*.

Lastly, identify your boundaries and start putting them into place in all of your relationships. This will help you keep true to yourself and not compromise.

LOVE LESSON 3

YOU IN THE RELATIONSHIP

CONGRATULATIONS! You've graduated from the two hardest Love Lessons in this book. It's time to lighten things up. Love Lesson # 3 is full of tips and tools to succeed in your quest to finding your one, as well as ways to prepare to *be* in your relationship.

Attracting your ideal partner is one thing, but making your relationship succeed is a whole other. That's because, as in any relationship, you will be tested by everyday nonsense that happens between two people sharing a life together. Knowing how to navigate through it with the tools you gain here will help you sustain a healthy, happy, long-term relationship.

I truly believe that without these tools, my own relationship with the man of my dreams would have been difficult, complicated, and challenging. I was lucky to have learned them, and now I hope to make it easier for you and your partner.

Let's start you off by making you a better dater.

7

THE ABCs
OF DATING

IF YOU REMEMBER only one rule about dating, make it this:
date to be known, not to be liked.

Dating is probably the part women struggle with the
most. Having been through it myself, I know dating isn't easy,
considering the emotional rollercoaster it can take us on...
the highs, the lows, the lies, the disappointments, the weir-
does... Omg, I could write a full book just on my own dating
experiences.

However, dating is part of the process to finding Mr. Right.
It's also one way you can put into practice everything you have
learned so far in this book, hopefully as a way to avoid repeating the same mistakes. That said, there are some serious
steps to follow to set yourself up for success instead of failure
when dating.

Let's get into it.

"But dating is such hard work."

If you want dating to be more fun instead of it feeling like a
chore, you need to change your attitude and perception on

how you go about dating. I would say that 90% of the women I interact with on a daily basis have a negative outlook on dating. If you are already going into it skeptically, how do you expect to attract any positive outcomes? To get the best experience you can from this process, you need to go into it with a positive frame of mind. This will make you more open to the people you meet and not shut out potential partners.

So, yes, dating can be frustrating, and yes, it is a lot of work. But you are looking for a life partner, not a roommate. He won't randomly show up at your door one day saying, "Hi, I'm your Mr. Right!" Ladies, you need to bite the bullet and go through the process, however it happens and however frustrating it may seem.

Think of it like shopping. When you're in the market to buy something new that will last over the long run, like a mattress, or that costs a crazy amount of money, like a condo or a new car, you shop around, don't you? You wouldn't do a spontaneous purchase without researching it, right? You'd go from dealership to dealership, taking that car on test drives, negotiating the best price, colour, model, etc. You would invest the time and do the work to make sure you get the best value.

If you desire love and a relationship for the right reasons, you need to put in the work, the effort. Things will change only when you decide to change your attitude on how you go about dating. Besides, exploring is part of the journey, and dating has many purposes. Learning to be a better dater will make your experiences much more fun.

With that in mind, let me share a couple of approaches you can try to put into practice to change your negative views on dating.

Two ways to change your views on dating

Don't be judgemental or have expectations

This is your absolute worst enemy. When we're in dating mode, the level of expectation we create in our heads towards people we haven't even met yet is scary. We haven't even gone on the date, yet we expect our date to show up and act a certain way towards us because we want results, and we want them fast.

This type of thinking can limit your dating options and prevent you from exploring new connections and experiences. By being too rigid with your expectations, you create opportunities to miss out on connecting with someone who could be a great match even if this person doesn't necessarily fit what you think is your ideal type. Get curious when dating, be open-minded and flexible, and most importantly be willing to get to know people as individuals. Let go of the need to have an outcome on any given date. Just go out and have fun.

*Side note: When you step out of your comfort zone and try something different, you might feel awkward while going through this "newness". Remember, this is essential for growth. Embrace the discomfort and allow yourself to learn and adapt to new experiences.

Be present in the moment

Don't worry about or try to propel yourself to the future. When we meet someone we like, we get caught up in the excitement, the romance, our desire to find our guy. We rush into it. We want it all to move fast. We so desperately want this (especially if the texting game has been hot and flirtatious). We create a fantasy in our minds that we want to come true. You know what? This is exactly where you can trip up and miss the necessary steps that are outlined a little later in this chapter.

You see, when we date, we only have one thing on our minds—finding the one. We haven't even gone on a date yet and we're already obsessing over that single-minded question (in its various forms), "Could he be the one? Is he the one? What if this is it?"

Sound familiar? I'm sure it does. We haven't even met this guy in person yet and we're already putting so much pressure on ourselves, never mind the pressure we put on the poor guy. I know I did it for years. We all do, even if we don't realize it. We project ourselves into the future, imagining rom-com scenarios in our heads, Disney endings...

But, ladies, they are NOT all potentials!

Remember, just because you meet a guy you click with, share similar interests with, and jive with in the few conversations you have before you meet, this doesn't necessarily mean he is a high-quality man for *you.*

Enjoy the moment for what it is—a moment. If it goes on, go with it.

Twelve steps to have a better date

Speaking of the moment, here are twelve steps you should follow and practice to make sure your dating experience is pleasant and successful.

1. Invest in your online dating profile

There is no way around this. If you are dating, chances are you're doing it online. If you are looking for a serious committed relationship, you should invest time on your profile. You are who you attract, so how you represent yourself matters. This includes everything from how you describe yourself, express what you are looking for, and how you present your-self in your pictures. Having a poorly set up profile out there is not a great way to start your dating journey. Set high stan-dards for yourself.

Check out a great video I created and posted on my IG channel with step-by-step details to follow to help you build your profile. You can find it at www.instagram.com/tv/CSNKT4Ypar2/

Just to be clear, online dating is not the only way to meet someone. So, if at this point you have already started doing these exercises and applying these methods, continue by say-ing yes to things; take every opportunity to be in situations where you can meet new people. You never know what might happen. Also, explore your network and actively tell them you are ready to meet someone so they know to think of you.

2. Take your time
Don't be in a rush. Be present. Things don't need to happen overnight. Remember, when you find your life partner you will have the rest of your life to experience, try, and do things together. Slow down and get to know someone adequately.

3. Practice the skills
Practice the skills you've identified in Chapters 5 and 6 to make sure you don't repeat the same patterns and old behaviours that haven't served you well in past relationships. Hopefully you have identified who you need to become going forward.

4. Be in observation mode
This one is my favourite. Men will say just about anything to get you. Words often mean nothing, while actions speak

volumes. Let him show you, not tell you. Just make sure you're looking and paying attention.

5. Pay attention to red flags

The quicker you notice these, the more time you will save yourself, not to mention the frustrations. Learn to trust your gut. You know that little voice that tells you something is not right? Pay attention to it! Stop trying to convince yourself or doubt that voice inside you when it speaks up. Excusing his behaviour or thinking you can change him is not the way to go.

6. Allow yourself to have fun

Dating should be exactly that ... FUN. It's a great way for you to play, to do activities you love to do. Get creative. You don't need to make a date about having dinner or coffee. If you are into sports, why not plan a bike ride, or a walk? Do things that interest you. It's also a great way to see how the person you are dating will react to the idea or be in these situations.

7. Ask quality questions

Remember that guy I dated who gave me the missing puzzle piece to discover my self-worth? How did it all start? Quality conversation. Ask quality questions, get quality answers (useless questions = useless answers). If he can't deliver on this simple equation, you know he's not the guy for you.

Just in case you're wondering, here are a few quality questions:

- What did you learn from your past relationship(s) and how did you grow from it?

- What books have you read that changed your life?

- What are the five core values you would like to pass on to your children?

- If you could change the world somehow, to heal it or make it better, how would that change look?

- Growing up, who had the greatest influence on you? Who was your greatest mentor?

- What do you love best about your relationship with your parents?

- What would your friends say about you? (The good and the bad.)

- What's a new skill you would like to gain?

- What do you think is one of your talents?

- What is on your bucket list in terms of travel/experiences/etc.?

8. Harness your feminine energy

Dating is a great way to connect to your divine feminine energy. Have some fun with your affirmations when looking at yourself in the mirror before you go out on a date. Wear the sexiest pair of underwear you have so you can know how hot you are underneath all those clothes. Put on a dress, and beautiful jewellery. Be adventurous with your make-up, curl your hair. You see where this is going. Let your date pamper and take care of you on your date. Flirt! There is nothing more attractive than a woman who feels confident about putting her flirt on.

9. Set your boundaries and state your needs from the beginning

If you've always struggled with putting yourself first, dating is a great opportunity to practice breaking that pattern. Don't be afraid to say what you want.

Here's an example:

If it's important for you to have your date pick you up, or call you instead of texting, say so. There is nothing wrong with sharing what is important to you or what you desire. It's actually better to do this right from the start, even after the first date, but in subtle ways. One thing at a time. You don't want to overwhelm the poor man.

You see, men are very simple creatures. They like things to be easy. However, they also need to know what they are in for from the beginning. If you start demanding and asking for all these things later, it will be too late. You need to do this when men are courting you.

If they are really into you, they will show up in all the ways you desire. If you wait too long, they will have time to change their minds after you have invested months, or sometimes a couple of years with them.

The longer you wait to say what's important to you, the more disappointed you can end up being. Or, worse, you could end up trying to turn him into someone he's not.

10. Be honest

If you are not into him or don't like certain things, be honest about it. We all need to get better at communicating how we feel, which includes stating clearly when we don't feel a connection with the other person. You are not responsible for his feelings, so don't be afraid to tell the truth. That being said, be very careful how you deliver the message. It should always be in a nice, genuine, loving way, the same way, I'm sure, you would appreciate receiving it yourself. There's nothing worse than being ghosted right? Let's break that bad habit by putting an end to it ourselves.

11. Let's talk about sex baby...
and about not doing it

It's as simple as that. I feel very strongly about this, and I know there are exceptions to the rules. But, when you're on a quest for a long-term committed relationship, this makes a huge difference in terms of the end results. Unless you are specifically looking for a one-night stand (which is more than OK), what's the rush? Sex is absolutely important in a relationship, but it's not everything. Your body is your temple, it is sacred. To give it away so easily without having built a form of trust between the two of you is just wrong. Your cookie needs to be earned! If a man is into you for the real and right reasons, he will wait. Not only that, but the build-up can turn out to be really exciting and fun. It's also something you can look forward to developing and working on together as a couple through the years. We've been taught so little about what sex means and what it is all about ... there is much more to it than just penetration (but that is a subject for a whole other book.)

12. Timing really is everything

If there is one thing I've learned over my years of singlehood, it is that timing is key. You could meet the right man at any given time, but if the timing isn't right, it might lead to nothing.

Jeff and I met at the right time. We both realized over the years we've been together that we had mutual acquaintances, had even been at a few of the same parties but never officially met. I know I would've never given him the time of day back then because I had decided this kind of man wasn't my type.

Life's crazy that way sometimes.

This is why I encourage you to work on yourself, to become the best version of yourself to receive the vision of the relationship and partner you have created.

ANA'S STORY

When I met Ana, she was in love with love. This made her an excellent candidate to rush into things quickly and compromise herself along the way to make sure she was "liked".

For so long, she felt she needed to appease the people she was dating and be easy-going, which often meant doing exactly what they wanted her to do. This translated into things happening faster than she wanted and her not being treated the way she truly desired to be treated. She also often ended up being friend zoned, consequently wasting her time. All this because she never communicated her needs from the beginning or held her partners accountable in any way because, again, she really wanted to be liked.

Through our work together, Ana learned that communicating her needs upfront and staying very clear about what she was looking for in a long-term relationship would help her avoid settling for anything that didn't resemble what she wanted. She also learned not to waste her time dating people with whom she felt no alignment, and as a result she was able to avoid dating burnout.

The other thing she realized she needed to change, which completely transformed her results in dating, was holding off on giving herself intimately too quickly (and also not getting drunk on dates).

"Holding myself in a more sacred position and not rushing into intimacy too soon was a key learning outcome. I was often confused, thinking the relationship was more than it actually was, especially when the sex was great. I'd then get blindsided, but still excuse behaviours I would normally never accept. It's given me a voice and it's allowed me to feel a lot stronger, clearer, and more connected to myself."

Ana learned the importance of communicating her needs, sticking to her boundaries, and keeping herself in an elevated, sacred space.

Summary

There you have it, the complete ABCs of dating to help you not only change your perspectives on dating, but also your attitude. If you follow these steps, especially about changing your mind on how you go about dating, you will absolutely have much more fun and see different results.

If you follow the twelve steps but still struggle, consider hiring a coach like myself and/or take one of my courses.

RAISE YOUR LOVE SIGNAL

1   Think about your last date; what was your thinking before you met the guy for the date? Were you already projecting yourself into the future? Were you already thinking he could be the "one"? If you answered yes to these questions, I want you to do some self-reflection and think about why you had this behaviour. Next time this happens, I want you to hear my voice in your head, reframe your thoughts, and be present in the moment.

2   Write down two things you need to do to improve your experience on your next date.

8

WHO YOU ARE IN
THE RELATIONSHIP

H OW CAN you make sure you stay true to who you are
in your relationship? Women often start a new relationship by pretending to be someone they are not, or
accommodate behaviours and things they normally wouldn't
because they really like the guy or want to be liked.

There is no reason to lose yourself. Relationships are
about two individuals who maintain their own lives and work
to create another one together. What if you knew from the
beginning that sacrifice doesn't need to be complicated or
detrimental to yourself? Couples are more likely to remain
in their relationship if both partners are willing to sacrifice for
each other and if that sacrifice comes with pre-set boundaries.

So why are we so afraid to state and stick to our boundaries right from the beginning? If we did that, we could avoid
disappointment and unmet expectations that lead to resentment and conflict. Establishing healthy boundaries allows
both partners to feel comfortable and develop a sense of
respect for one another. Remember the lesson from Chapter
6; in order to establish boundaries, you need to be clear with
your partner about who you are, what you want, your beliefs,
values, and limits.

Stay true to who YOU are

Once you have identified what you want, what you need, and who you need to become to get it, let's make sure you don't lose yourself along the way. It can be easy to step into self-doubt when you have been single for a long time, looking for that partner, and constantly hearing from your entourage things like "Why are you still single? You're probably too demanding." Or "You're too intimidating. Are you sure you're not being too picky and difficult?" Or one of my favourites, "What is your problem?"

Does this sound familiar? These words can make you not only doubt who you are, but they can influence you to the point of settling on your needs and wants.

This happened to me. I started doubting who I was and often questioned myself, particularly asking if my standards were too high. I even toned down my strong personality with the men I dated because I was told I was too intimidating. I stepped out of being my true authentic self because of what people around me told me.

How in the world did I let myself get caught up with what other people thought was right for me? Ladies, nobody knows you like you do. Letting other people dictate what is right or wrong for you just doesn't work. When I started listening to myself instead, I stepped into my power and owned who I am like never before.

"The right man for me will embrace me as I am, 100%," I told myself.

Today, I am in a relationship with a man who not only embraces my strong and big personality, he also admires it. So, let me save you the years it took me to understand this: Listen and trust only yourself, and never forget that nobody knows you like you do.

That's one way to ensure you stay true to yourself. Another is not allowing yourself to try to change in the process of building a relationship. As women, we easily compromise (a.k.a. change) who we are to accommodate the men who come in and out of our lives. Especially when we are desperately seeking our dream relationship. We get caught up in the moment, or the fantasy in our heads telling us this is exciting, convincing ourselves that "This is it! This is my guy! I have found love!" Then, slowly, we begin to ignore the red flags, telling ourselves that he will change, or better yet, that we will change him.

We are afraid to share what we truly want. We dim our own light to make our partner comfortable or to accommodate his insecurities.

When I question my clients about their failed relationships, I ask these questions:

- Now that you look back, did you see the red flags at the beginning?

- Did you convince yourself he would change with time?

- Did you choose to ignore your inner voice telling you something is not right?

Guess what?

They all say "Yes!" That's because we always know. We hear that little voice inside, but we choose to ignore it by getting caught up in the fantasy and the romance of things.

Case study: A lesson hard come by

When I initially met Rachelle, she had been with her boyfriend for two years. He had cheated on her numerous times and shamed her for being successful in her business. He wouldn't support her career. He wanted to keep her under his control. Following our sessions together, she finally had the courage to leave him even though she desperately wanted to get married.

The story didn't end there. Six weeks later, he finally proposed, promising he would stay loyal, support her in her business, and give her the wedding she had always dreamed of. This blindsided her because of her lack of self-confidence and self-worth.

She forgot to pay attention to the red flags, ignoring the fundamental pillars required to be in a healthy relationship, such as respect, trust, and acceptance of the other. She got caught up in the romance, convincing herself he would change or had changed (somehow in less than six weeks!). She got married for the wrong reasons. Sadly, within eighteen months, she found herself getting divorced. She had never developed her eagle-eyed vision, the bigger picture.

Eagle-eyed vision

As I mentioned in Love Lessons 1 and 2, if you take the time to get clear on your wants and needs, and learn what your boundaries are and practice applying them, it will be that much easier for you to develop what I call "eagle vision".

The eagle has the strongest vision in the entire animal kingdom. It has 20/5 vision compared to the average human, who only has 20/20 vision[6]. Eagle vision represents a higher perspective and keen perceptions using our intuitive senses. Basically, it means you stay focused on what really matters, see the bigger picture, and consider the long-term vision

---

6   "Eagle Eye." *Wikipedia*, Wikimedia Foundation. https://en.wikipedia.org/wiki/Eagle_eye.

instead of the short one. This means you won't get blindsided by the butterflies, the lust, the amazing sex, or the simple excitement of meeting someone new you really like.

After doing all of the work I outlined in this book myself (yes, I practice what I preach), I looked back at every short-term fling and relationship I had been involved in. I recognized that I had never, ever stayed true to who I was with any of these men until I met my current partner.

Can you imagine? So much work pretending to be someone I was not.

What I had never realized was that I was the biggest part of the problem. How can you be in a healthy, loving, and honest relationship if you are not even being the real you? After all, the goal is to be loved and accepted for who you are, don't you think?

Why would you ever want to be in a relationship in which you have to tolerate things you typically wouldn't, pretend to like things you don't, or hide opinions and adopt beliefs you do not agree with? This will not only set you up to fail, it will also sabotage the actual relationship.

When I started dating my fiancé, I made a promise to myself that I would not only stay true to who I was but I would also remain every bit me, including the good and the bad. I communicated my boundaries and did not compromise myself or my beliefs in any form.

I can attest that it is the greatest feeling in the world to be myself in every shape and way and be accepted for it. I never feel I have to dim my light, or hide things, pretend, or like something I don't. On the contrary, my partner supports, encourages, and loves all of my quirkiness, my idiosyncrasies, and so on. He honours and respects me. He loves me, for all of me.

What a truly amazing situation to be in.

Your role in the relationship

In a relationship, there are two people. It's not just about *you*, *your* wants, and *your* needs. Everything needs to be reciprocated. As we explore how *to be* in a relationship, keep in mind that everything here applies to the two of you.

Most relationships fail because:

- We pretend to be someone we're not or accept things we typically wouldn't.

- We do not take the time to communicate our needs and wants from the beginning.

- We assume our partners should read our minds.

- We keep everything bottled up when we don't get what we want, the way we want it, which builds resentment to a point of no return.

- There is an imbalance between the two partners in terms of how they serve each other (One always feels they do more than the other.)

- We try to change our partners.

- We have unrealistic expectations.

For any relationship to work, evolve, and grow, there needs to be an agreement, a mutual willingness and desire to serve each other's needs, wants, and general happiness. You each need to take ownership of your role in the relationship. However, we often fall into the trap of taking each other for granted, or we get lazy in our actions and get caught up in our own self-absorbed needs. We focus on what our partners *aren't* doing instead of remembering why we came together in the first place, that is, to mutually take care of each other's needs, wants, and happiness.

That's why it is important to get clear on your *why*. Why do you want to be in a relationship? Are these really the right reasons? Are you ready to do the work it actually takes to make the relationship succeed and last? Everything in this book aims to show you how to do things differently once and for all to succeed. If you do, you will not only change your perspective on everything you thought love and being in a relationship was all about, but you will also attract love and succeed in your relationship like you never thought possible.

Fundamental pillars

I want to elaborate more on the fundamental pillars you need to build on and maintain to have a life-story relationship (I'll explain this concept in the next chapter). I personally apply these every day to make sure my relationship stays healthy. It's been a game changer for both of us and how we each show up for our relationship.

Here are six I want to share with you. Please don't take the attached numbers as a rating. All the pillars are equally important to nourish, cultivate, and practice.

1. Willingness
You must have the willingness to listen, to communicate, to have difficult conversations, and to focus on the solution and not the problem. The willingness to compromise and not let your egos get in the way. To want to mutually take care of each other's needs and wants. The willingness to make things work when they're not working and to be mutually 100% invested, without having one partner more invested than the other.

Finally, the willingness to hold each other to high standards and always put the relationship first (seems like a simple task, but it's much easier said than done). You *both* must care and hold each other accountable at all times.

2. Respect

Respect is the cornerstone of any healthy relationship. When you have respect for one another, you understand each other's needs, wants, and mindsets. It means you each respect the other for who you are, and you truly love each other for it. You both recognize that you are individuals with different opinions and experiences, and that that is OK. Respect means you don't feel the need to change or affirm their thoughts or belief systems to align with yours. You don't challenge the boundaries each has set or ever cross the line when things don't work out.

Respect shows up in how we seek to understand each other when we actually don't, how we express empathy for our differences, how we apologize when we're wrong, how we show gratitude for each other, how polite we are with each other, and, my favourite, how we actively listen versus doing so passively. Active listening in a relationship requires you to be present in the conversation instead of trying to prove the other wrong or make your own point.

Respect requires honesty and loyalty from both parties. When this pillar is mutually practiced, it creates room for the relationship to grow and stay very healthy. When we love our partners, and they love us, we want what is best for us both.

3. Acceptance

Lack of acceptance is one of the reasons relationships fail. We try to change our partners. Instead, learn to accept your partner's behaviours and patterns from the beginning and don't try to change them. Trying to make him become who he is not, and probably wasn't from the beginning, is a big no-no.

I'm sure many of you ladies can identify with this example: he's never great at remembering key dates or writing a birthday card. Every year you hope he'll remember, but he doesn't. Because *that's not who he is.*

Then again, maybe he's great at making dinner when you work late, or doing the laundry, or making breakfast for the kids on weekends while you sleep in.

I am obsessive about making my bed first thing in the morning. However, my dear fiancé typically gets up later than I do, and never does the bed. It drives me crazy! I've tried to change this bad habit … but that's just not who he is and I am OK with that.

On the flipside, my man is super obsessive about having a clean kitchen sink. I tend to leave it dirty with a bunch of stuff in there. It drives him crazy! I've tried to get better at it, but I am not going to change. We've both accepted each other's quirks. I make the bed if I want it to look nice, he cleans the sink. We've accepted our little differences and crack jokes about it. We've made it playful and laugh about it instead of getting frustrated.

Note: Acceptance does not only apply to the big things. It's especially important with the little things. Nothing kills a relationship faster than focusing on the meaningless stuff. ☺ Make sure you focus on what he does well, instead of trying to change him and the things he doesn't do as well.

4. Thoughtfulness

As already mentioned, it's easy to start taking each other for granted as time goes by. We forget to do the "thoughtful" things we did so easily for each other at the beginning of the relationship. When we start dating, we always look for ways to impress, take care of, or please the other person in our courting process. We want to make them happy, right?

But then, with time, we get lazy. We forget to...

- greet each other at the door when one comes home,

- plan dates,

- pick our partner up at the airport when they travel,

- wear nice underwear like we used to,

- shave our legs to be well groomed for our man,

- remember special dates or anniversaries that are important to our partner,

- hold hands and be affectionate.

This is where frustration and resentment can build up, when we think, "Why don't we do that anymore?" We let our standards and the desire to make our partners happy dissipate with time when they should actually get stronger. Imagine how relationships would thrive if we cultivated this thoughtfulness with time instead of giving it all away in the beginning and then slowly eliminating it.

This could be a game changer in the quality of our long-term relationships. But, it won't always be easy. It requires both of you to make those additional efforts. It also takes a commitment to keep each other to high standards in the relationship, which is why you both need the "willingness" mentioned above as a key pillar.

5. Communication

When communication is properly applied, it can get you through anything. Communication is the key to success in all your relationships. It's become a very important part of my coaching sessions.

I used to be the worst communicator because, like most of us, I had never been taught how to do it. I only got good at it in my forties. Through my self-development journey and the issues I experienced thanks to my lack of communication skills, I set a goal for myself to start learning how to develop this vital skill. I worked at it ... hard!

It paid off. I've become an excellent communicator not only in my relationships, but with my friends, my clients, and in any situation where conflict arises. I even train corporate staff to use my mastermind techniques on how to communicate in the workplace. If you are not great at it, you can still develop this skill. Anyone can.

So, what is communicating?

Communicating is a means to express our ideas, our thoughts, and our feelings to someone else. It's the act or process of using words, signs, sounds, or behaviours to exchange information.

But here is the key: Communicating is making sure you and the recipient each understands the information shared. You can communicate all day long with someone, but if they don't understand you, then you haven't communicated anything.

So how can you make sure to understand and be understood? Well, consider this first: Don't make assumptions about the person in front of you, that is, don't assume that he or she 'should know' or 'should understand' everything you are saying and expressing. We each think and interpret things differently. Hoping that people can read our minds is just wrong.

Keep in mind that we have been raised differently, taught differently, experienced life differently. So why would we expect people to think as we do? Take ownership of your communication to clearly express your needs and desires to your partner. That is *your* responsibility.

6. Tenderness

When I think of tenderness, I close my eyes, put my hand on my heart, and allow myself to experience feelings of safety, being taken care of, supported. I thoroughly let the woman in me be taken care of by my man without feeling any threat or unwanted condition. I feel loved.

It fills up my whole being. It's a feeling of peace and emotional connection. When you mutually exchange feelings of tenderness with one another, it helps activate thoughtfulness and empathy. You will always want what is best for your partner without focusing on your self-absorbed needs, which can often surface once we get too comfortable in our relationship.

Summary

Are you ready to give what you are asking to receive?

You are enough as you are. You are awesome, you are beautiful, you are not "too much". You deserve all the love you've ever dreamed of and you especially deserve to be loved for all of you. Continue being the amazing person you are, keep learning, evolving, and growing, and most of all, never, ever dim your light. The right person will see you shining bright from afar. And, don't forget, you want to be accepted for all of you, but this is not a one-way street.

Remember the six key pillars that can make any relationship successful. However, for all of them to succeed, they have to be reciprocated. There cannot be an imbalance wherein one partner gives only 50%. It has to 100% from both sides at all times.

Get familiar with and learn to apply the six fundamental pillars to your relationship. They are game changers. Hold each other accountable to high standards in your relationship and learn to put what is best for the relationship first.

RAISE YOUR LOVE SIGNAL

Going into any relationship, learning to stay true to who you are is a key element to success. Ask yourself the questions, "Who is the true me? Can I be me and stay me?"

Do you even know the answers to these questions? Write yourself a letter telling yourself who you are. It is a very powerful exercise.

Also, identify what is important to you that you want your partner to accept and respect. Make a list.

Finally, start applying and mastering the six fundamental pillars in every relationship you have. This will help you succeed in your relationship once you have found your match.

9

BEING IN THE
RELATIONSHIP

NOW, LET'S DIVE into a few basics of what makes a healthy, long-term, committed relationship. Because it's one thing to attract the right partner, but succeeding in your relationship is another.

We tend to think that once we have found our person, we can kick back, relax, and enjoy the ride. For relationships to grow and evolve in a healthy way, they need work, investment, and nurturing. However, because we've never been taught what love is really all about and how "to be" in a relationship, we go into them blind, convinced that love will be enough.

But I am here to tell you, love is not enough. (I know, it sucks, right?) Think about it; our idea of love is based on how we have been programmed to think about it, the Disney-fied, rom-comed concept played out. We are in love with the idea of being "in love". The feeling, not the action.

That's not to say that a life filled with romance and significant magical moments like getting engaged, married, having kids, buying a house, planning vacations, and the rest isn't absolutely part of the great adventure. But, it is also much more than that.

A long-term relationship comes with the ups and downs of everyday life, the daily stress, finances, challenges, feeling tired, not seeing eye-to-eye on everything, kids, and just plain being individuals going through our own issues.

Knowing how to navigate the hardships is what really matters to make the relationship last in a healthy way. It's a lot to handle if you don't have a solid foundation built up already. And the butterflies you experienced when you first met, the spontaneous nights out, the feelings of wanting to be with your partner 24/7, and the hot passionate sex? These will come and go. As will that feeling of being in love.

If we were told in advance what a long-term relationship or marriage actually means, wouldn't you think twice about choosing your partner wisely and make better decisions? Or, at the very least you would make sure you had the tools to grow in your relationship together and know how to handle obstacles instead of giving up, not communicating how you feel, not acknowledging your partner's needs, all the while building resentment and frustration.

I truly feel if we were taught these things beforehand, our relationships would be handled differently:

- We would pick our partners more wisely and for the right reasons.

- We would focus on the actions of love versus the feelings of love.

- We would have healthier love lives and a chance at more success in long-term relationships.

- We would know to put the relationship before anything and everything else. "We" would come first.

My hope is to eventually hear from you with your successful stories in your own relationships as you put these ideas and lessons into practice. It has completely transformed how I see, act, and behave in mine. It sure has made it a happy place.

Just to be clear, my relationship isn't perfect. But, having the toolbox I have built over the years and the awareness of everything I talk about in this book has completely transformed how I choose to show up in my relationship.

Love is a beautiful thing and life is too short to be spent in continuous cycles of unhappiness and in not allowing yourself to love, or be loved. Instead, start cultivating healthy habits to ensure you can both be happy together and as individuals. This starts with thinking not only about "I" or "me", but also "us".

Life story vs. love story

In my readings, I once stumbled across these very wise words from the famous relationship expert Esther Perel:

"Love is a verb. It's not a permanent state of enthusiasm. It's not about finding the right person; it's about being the right person. If you just want to be dazzled, then you will have an adventure. You will have a love story, but you won't have a life story. And a life story is different from a love story."

She was so right, and this totally opened my eyes to a whole new way of seeing things. We've been trained to think of and to desire a "love story", not a "life story". You need to decide which of these kinds of relationships you want to have. They don't come with the same set of values, deal-breakers, and needs. Hence, the importance of getting crystal clear on everything outlined in this book:

- Your needs in a relationship and what really matters to you

- Not looking for outside validation for your happiness

- Loving yourself first

- Stating your boundaries and sticking to them

- Staying true to who you are and not pretending to be someone you are not

- Mastering the fundamental pillars for a successful relationship

- Remembering to always put the relationship first

And finally, learning how "to be" in a relationship, as we'll discuss now.

First of all, let's be clear that you can have romance and passion in your life story. If it's anything like I've experienced, these things grow with time. Jeff and I both decided to invest in *us* and hold each other to high standards in our relationship.

For once in my life, I had decided to do things differently. Every single "love story" I had experienced, with all the passion, lust, and fairy tales, failed. I finally realized that what I truly needed was a relationship that was safe, secure, stable, and supportive. I needed to be with someone whom I could grow and evolve with as an individual and as a couple. My needs were very clear. I needed the life story.

It has been a refreshing experience. I am more in love with my man today, four years later, than I was the first year we dated. We have grown to love each other at a very different level and to invest in creating magic and romance whenever we want, instead of letting all of it happen at the beginning. So, instead of the fireworks at the start, which quickly dissipate with the years, we reversed the way we light up our fire, and it's something we've cultivated and worked hard at together, consistently.

So how does this apply to you? Let me outline the simple basics you can start putting into place and even start practicing in the variety of relationships you have.

(Note: If you want to learn even more about how to be in a relationship, sign up for one of my courses or stay tuned for my next book, which will comprehensively explore *being* in a relationship.)

Where to start

First off, pace yourself. It's important to take your time as you settle into your new relationship.

Develop that mindset, the one that tells you that you have all the time in the world to do, explore, and experience the numerous things you always dreamed of, desired, and fantasized about, together. Just remind yourself regularly that it's about being and staying in a relationship for the right reasons, that there is no need to rush into anything. Think about it, everything we do in life and that we want to become good at, takes time and effort. This is not a sprint, it's a marathon.

Take your alone time

Don't give up everything and everyone you had in your life pre-relationship. Of course, it is important to have common interests as a couple, but it is equally important for each of you to have your own life and individuality. Whether that means hanging out with friends, doing sports, travelling, taking time alone, or pursuing your passions, keep these going. Don't forget that you were individuals before you were a couple.

I've witnessed this many times amongst friends and I am sure you can relate; your best friend falls in love and is out-of-this-world excited about her new beau or his new gal. You, being a good friend, understand and support this happiness. However, you start seeing less and less of your friend, until you almost never see her (or him).

People lose themselves. They lose their personal identity because they get wrapped up in the love bubble, the *feeling* of love I referred to earlier. It's like a feeling of urgency to do, live, and experience everything right now.

I get it. That feeling is addictive. It activates our serotonin levels (our happiness hormones), so who the hell wouldn't want to eat all of that up right away (I've been that girl, too). When we do this, though, we also skip those beneficial steps, like enjoying the present moment instead of propelling ourselves into the future, keeping the foreplay going for a year instead of a month or two, forgiving or accepting things we typically wouldn't because we are feeling the love (You know the famous saying, "love is blind"? Well, it's no lie.)

There are a lot of great reasons to make sure you spend time alone and not forget who you were as individuals pre-relationship, including:

- Staying sexy and independent in our partners' eyes. (Our crazy minds love what we can't have, so more time apart creates desire.)

- Creating new dynamic conversations. (This is especially important when you have been in a relationship five- or ten-plus years.)

- Appreciating each other more. It's often when we take a step back that we realize the value of our partner and our relationship.

- Feeling happier and fulfilled internally instead of relying on someone else for your happiness. (Which can also lighten the burden on your partner if you have those expectations.)

- Avoiding neediness, especially if you are an Anxious attachment style.

Jeff and I love to be together, but we also love our time apart. We both need our "me" time and we both need time with our respective friends.

It doesn't need to be a whole week or a weekend. Sometimes, a simple evening makes a world of difference. I can watch my girly shows that he hates, spend time with my girls talking about whatever, or do a full home spa with no distractions. Just some time apart.

Funnily enough, every time I take my time alone, I get excited to reconnect. I miss him. I am more patient, I don't snap, and I'm more attentive to my man. It's great.

Don't forget who mattered in your life pre-relationship. Continue making time for yourself and the things that fulfill you.

Be reciprocal

Earlier, I talked about how to be your true authentic self and about being loved for all of who you are, and who you are not. Well, that applies to the other side of the fence as well. If you want to be treated a certain way, it needs to be reciprocated.

Accepting and respecting each other for who you both are is non-negotiable, from the beginning and throughout the partnership. Take note of these words carefully because you will catch yourself trying to change your partner at one point or another in your relationship. (It still happens to me.)

You have to honour each other's differences and embrace them. Remind yourself who you fell in love with at the start. Besides, the only way anyone changes is if they decide they want to change themselves. You will be in a constant state of frustration and disappointment if you convince yourself otherwise.

Managing expectations

This is a major issue. That's because we tend to expect things from the people we love. We assume that our partners should know everything we want and need because they are our partners.

But guess what? No matter how close and connected you might feel to your partner, no one reads minds. You are the only one responsible for creating and experiencing the disappointment that will follow unmet expectations, not your partner. When our expectations are not managed, they can become a vicious cycle causing numerous misunderstandings and even worse, resentment. There is no such thing as justified resentment. It will only destroy you and your relationship.

Unless, that is, you have taken the time to clearly communicate your needs and wants. Then it becomes a whole other conversation.

To be fair, there are still times I have expectations that are not met in my relationship because I didn't say what I wanted. However, I try to catch myself now. I've learned to reframe my frustrations within myself rather than take it out on my partner because it is my own fault for not sharing them.

Here are four tips you can apply to help you manage expectations—by the way, I apply these techniques not only with my partner, but also with meaningful relationships I have with my friends and family. It's really helped resolve issues quickly instead of hanging on to anger, disappointment, frustration, and resentment.

1. Don't assume your partner can read your mind
He/she can't. Thinking otherwise is just wrong.

2. Communicate your needs
Since no one can read your mind, learn to say out loud what you want or need. Be clear and assertive in doing so.

3. Watch your attitude
Don't punish your partner with an attitude because you didn't get what you wanted. They should not have to pay for something you assumed they should have known. Own your mistake.

4. Observe, don't react
When you get triggered, take a step back. Don't automatically react. Ask yourself, "Why am I being triggered right now? Is it really my partner's fault? Did I take the time to communicate what I wanted and needed?"

4a. Out of body experience (I've integrated this practice in my life and it does wonders.)
You will get triggered and occasionally feel frustrated or unhappy with something not happening or going the way you want. When this happens, do the following:

a   Take a deep breath and remove yourself temporarily from the situation.

b   Ask yourself, "How is my attitude, my frustration, or my comment in this situation going to serve the relationship? Will it help in any way or create more conflict?"

These questions remove you from the emotional drama and calm the ego. You'll quickly come to realize that 98% of the time the answer to the last question is "No". The need to be right, even when you are wrong, will set you up for failure and a constant feeling of discontentment. Focus on the solution, not the problem. Focusing on the problem won't solve or serve the situation.

Learn to argue without the emotional drama

There is nothing wrong with having arguments in our relationships, but how we navigate and deal with them is important. Who responds well to screams and anger in the heat of the moment? No one. We go into a defensive mode, shut down, and say or otherwise express things we don't really mean.

When you do get into an argument, even if it's just a simple disagreement, speak from a place of how you feel about the situation. Don't blame or accuse. Have a mindset that focuses on the solution, not the problem. Begin the conversation with "I felt this way."

Here's an example:

Your hubby forgot your wedding anniversary.

"I felt hurt and unappreciated when our anniversary went unnoticed. I was disappointed and sad because our anniversary means a lot to me."

Or, he shows up late for your date:

"When you don't show up on time to our date, it makes me feel unimportant or dismissed."

And from the receiver's end:

"I'm sorry I disappointed you. I'd like us to find a way to make special occasions more memorable for both of us."

Or

"I'm sorry to hear that I make you feel this way. It wasn't my intention."

Also, keep these tips in mind:

- **Listen:** Are you listening to respond and fight back or are you present in the conversation? Are you listening and judging at the same time? Be present. Pay attention to the moment and to what your partner is sharing with you.

- **Acknowledge:** When we are upset about something, we want our partner to hear us out, right? Acknowledging your partner's pain will immediately defuse their frustration or anger. Say something like "I understand/hear what you are saying." Try apologizing if the moment calls for it: "I'm sorry I made you feel that way," or "I am sorry you are frustrated."

- **Let go of the need to be right:** Understand each other's perspectives. Being wrong or right in any given argument won't serve the relationship in any way. Ask yourself, "Is this really worth the argument? Will it serve the relationship?"

- **Seek resolution:** After expressing your feelings, focus on finding the solution you can both agree with. "What can we do to make sure this situation doesn't happen again?"

Applying these simple techniques will transform your arguments to healthy ones and help resolve conflict much faster.

One last note. If you are in the heat of the argument and don't yet know how to express your thoughts clearly, say so: "I need time," or "Let me put my thoughts together." Respect each other's need for the time out.

I do, however, recommend you cap that time period and revisit the situation sooner rather than later. These tips aren't meant to be a free ticket to avoid the conversation and sweep the situation under the rug. Try circling back within twenty-four hours.

Summary

Are you ready to invest in and work on your relationship? A relationship is a full-time job. You both need to hold each other to high standards from the beginning. If you do not perform and give your best on a regular basis, you could lose the job. Get intentional in your relationship after the honeymoon phase. Take your time and don't forget who you were before the relationship. Make sure to accept your partner for who he is instead of trying to change him. Be mindful and manage your expectations, and master the art of communicating and arguing without the emotional drama.

Incorporating kindness and thoughtfulness into your dynamic will take you further. And last, always put the relationship first—move from *me* to *we*.

RAISE YOUR LOVE SIGNAL

Next time you seriously start dating someone, ask yourself these questions:

1   Are you rushing into things?

2   Are you tossing everything aside just to focus on this new person?

3   Are you catching yourself trying to change him or convincing yourself he will change with time?

Remind yourself to slow down and remember your "eagle vision".

Do not get caught up in making the other person wrong and yourself right (no ego!)

Develop your communication skills (take my master-class) by visiting raiseyourlovesignal.com/free-masterclass/

Learn how to be in a relationship before going into a relationship.

CONCLUSION

As WE HAVE seen throughout this book, Attracting and Keeping the Love of Your Life is not a simple journey, but it is achievable. It is about finding that new way to go about our quest to find love and ensuring the quality of the relationship we desire.

So, what did we discuss? Let's review.

Love Lesson #1—Your Wants

Take the time to create your vision of the relationship you desire. Get crystal clear on what you want, what you need from a partner, and what you need from the actual relationship. Understand the difference between needs and wants so you can identify what really matters to you. Have clarity on your deal-breakers and your *why* in wanting to be in a relationship.

Love Lesson #2—Your Self

Understanding where you're coming from is a key element in your journey to attracting the right partner and being in a healthy relationship. This requires a lot of self-reflection and deep discovery to understand the roots of who you are and why you are the way you are. It will also reveal why and how you show up, or not, in your relationships.

Love Lesson #3—You in the Relationship

Become a regular dater and practice all the skills you have honed so that you do not repeat the same mistakes and eventually you will attract a high-quality match. Before finding the relationship you have been waiting for, make sure you know how to nurture it once you're in it. This includes staying true to who you are, managing your expectations, and becoming a great communicator who can express your needs and manage conflict.

The one thing I would urge you to practice, be it in your dating experiences or in any area of your life, is to *be open*, to try something new, and to explore, change, and think differently. Don't limit yourself, or your accessibility, by staying stuck in your ways, doing the same things over and over again. In my own case, I truly believe this has been the catalyst for the growth I have experienced and everything I have accomplished, including finding love and a healthy committed relationship. You will certainly get results much more quickly.

Knowing what I know today, I wish I'd been taught these things at a younger age. This is not to say I would've necessarily understood and applied all of the lessons, but it would've definitely helped me avoid such a long period of time lacking self-worth, having doubts, suffering and believing I could never be loved for who I was. It would've also helped me leave hard situations or relationships sooner because I would have had the self-awareness to recognize they weren't working, why they weren't working, and how to do things differently and better.

If you do the work, you will not only attract your partner, but you will experience love at a whole other level that you never thought possible. And, to your biggest surprise, it might not even be in a relationship but with yourself first.

The information in this book is not easy to digest, practice, or apply. However, if you want to have different results from what you have been getting so far and attract high-quality relationships, you have to do the work, elevate your thinking process, and be a better version of yourself. I truly hope this book helps you Raise Your Love Signal, whether that is with yourself or your new beau.

We all deserve love. The road to finding it is not always easy, but it is definitely possible. If you are struggling, get help or support. I wouldn't be where I am today or learned everything I have without the numerous teachers and coaches I have worked with.

Let's stop thinking therapy should only happen when we hit rock bottom or have problems. When I talk about therapy, it doesn't need to be with a therapist or a psychologist. It can be with a coach, a course, a conference, or even a good read. Anytime we want to learn something new or become better at a certain skill, we seek help. Why wouldn't we do this with important things like love, dating, and relationships?

Do anything you can to help improve yourself, develop your self-awareness, understand who you are and why you are the way you are. Understand your mistakes and the patterns you keep repeating. Be proactive instead of reactive. Develop a toolbox of amazing skills to help you deal with difficult times.

Flourish

There are such great resources out there. Be open, be an avid learner, and continuously improve yourself. Love is the most powerful and peaceful feeling to experience. I wish this for you all.

NEXT STEPS

IF YOU WANT to continue the conversation on how to find your life partner and expand your knowledge of yourself and how to be in a relationship, please visit my website for my numerous services and courses: www.raiseyourlovesignal.com.

Join one of my group coaching programs, and/or take one of my courses:
"Learn how to be in relationship before being in relationship"
"The art of communicating in relationships"

Apply to work with me one on one.

Hire me to speak at your event.

Let's Wine about Love (private events)

Join my community.

Stay tuned for Book # 2—*Raise Your Love Signal: How to Keep the Fire Burning in Your Relationship*

SUGGESTED READINGS

Brené Brown, *Daring Greatly: How the Courage to Be Vulnerable Transforms the Way We Live, Love, Parent, and Lead*

Don Miguel Ruiz, *The Four Agreements, A Practical Guide to Personal Freedom*

Gabor Matè, *The Myth of Normal: Trauma, Illness & Healing in a Toxic Culture*

Gary Chapman, *The 5 Love Languages: The Secret to Love that Lasts*

H. Norman Wright, *101 Questions to Ask Before You Get Engaged*

Harville Hendrix (PhD), and Helen LaKelly Hunt, (PhD), *Getting the Love You Want: A Guide for Couples, 3rd ed.*

Jess McCann, *If Love Is A Blessing, Why Do I Feel Cursed?: Overcome The Sabotaging Habits You Never Knew You Had & Get The Relationship You've Always Wanted*

Joe Dispenza, *Breaking the Habit of Being Yourself*

Miriam Ribiat, *I Wish Someone Would Have Told Me*

Stan Tatkin, *Wired for Love: How Understanding Your Partner's Brain and Attachment Style Can Help You Defuse Conflict and Build a Secure Relationship*

Wayne W. Dyer, *I Can See Clearly Now*

Winfrey, Oprah, and Bruce Perry, *What Happened to You?: Conversations on Trauma, Resilience, and Healing*

ACKNOWLEDGMENTS

FIRST AND FOREMOST, I would like to thank the amazing man I share my life with, Jeff. You make me the best student of my own teachings daily. Thank you for your support, encouragement, patience, and interest while I wrote this book. You were often my sounding board, helping me talk through things I was trying to put into words. Without knowing it, you are the reason I am writing this book. Thank you for showing me what love and being in a healthy relationship are all about. I never imagined I could experience such a safe, loving space with someone.

I want to thank all the men that have come in and out of my life, good or bad as I have learned so much through it all. I never would've become who I am today without every single one of you. It's a beautiful thing to be able to look back and understand why things happened the way they did (or didn't) and be at peace with it.

I would like to thank the incredible women I have around me, who have participated in more ways than one through the process of bringing this book to life.

Melissa—You have taken our meaning of BFFs to a whole other level with your words of encouragement through my numerous breakdowns and support as I birthed this project.

Miriam,Tanya, Deb: our brainstorm sessions with wine, laughter, and your words of support and encouragement. I couldn't have made it without you.

Paulo, for your "Genius".

Special thanks to Stacey Russell who actually helped me birth the vision and name Raise Your Love Signal.

I would also like to thank my peeps that took the time to read the book pre-launch. Your valid time and feedback helped make sure this book is as solid as it is in my head.

My writing coach, Siobhan. Your guidance and encouragement and you're keeping me accountable on delivery made it so much easier for me to keep pounding through.

The famous saying—it takes a village. It really does. I couldn't have accomplished any of this without the amazing community and support system around me.

REFERENCES

"John Bowlby." *Wikipedia*, Wikimedia Foundation, 23 July 2023, en.wikipedia.org/wiki/John_Bowlby.

Brown, Levine, Amir, and Rachel Heller. *Attached: The New Science of Adult Attachment and How It Can Help You Find—and Keep—Love*. Jeremy P. Tarcher/Penguin, 2010.

Perel, Esther. *Mating in Captivity: Unlocking Erotic Intelligence*. Harper, 2006.

Merriam-Webster. "Webster's Dictionary." *Merriam-Webster*, 2021, www.merriam-webster.com/dictionary.

The Attachment Project. "Four Attachment Styles." www.attachmentproject.com/blog/four-attachment-styles/.

Winfrey, Oprah. "Oprah's Gratitude Journal: Oprah on Gratitude." Oprah.com. Accessed November 13, 2023. https://www.oprah.com/spirit/oprahs-gratitude-journal-oprah-on-gratitude.

ABOUT THE AUTHOR

CHANTAL LANDREVILLE is a Certified Love & Relationship Coach with over two decades of experience in the realm of personal growth and human connection. She has been offering her programs to women, men, and couples for the last four years.

She is on a mission to guide us towards a new way of viewing our rapport with love, dating, and relationships to make sure we can experience healthier, deeper human connections.

She aims to integrate the social skills training required to survive in this crazy world, such as emotional intelligence, self-confidence/worth, and communication skills, into school curricula. The earlier these subjects are taught, the more aware and prepared young adults will be to succeed in their relationships, including with themselves.

"Love conquers all" (37 B.C.) by Roman poet Virgil.

After writing this book, and going through one hell of a journey of Love, Chantal can confirm this is indeed true.

Social media

Instagram   @chantal.landreville

Facebook   Raise Your Love Signal group

TikTok   @chantalryls

LinkedIn   www.linkedin.com/in/
chantal-landreville-74358910/

Website   raiseyourlovesignal.com

Scan the code below for direct links and contact form: